The Old West in the Old World

The Old West in the Old World

WORLD

LOST PLAYS
by Bret Harte and Sam Davis

Edited by LAWRENCE I. BERKOVE
and GARY SCHARNHORST

University of New Mexico Press / Albuquerque

© 2006 by the University of New Mexico Press
All rights reserved. Published 2006
Printed in the United States of America
10 09 08 07 06   1 2 3 4 5

LIBRARY OF CONGRESS CATALOGING-IN-PUBLICATION DATA

Harte, Bret, 1836–1902.
    [Luck of Roaring Camp]
    The Old West in the old world : lost plays by Bret Harte and Sam Davis / edited by Lawrence I. Berkove and Gary Scharnhorst.
    p. cm.
    Includes index.
    ISBN-13: 978-0-8263-3764-1 (alk. paper)
    ISBN-10: 0-8263-3764-3 (alk. paper)
1. West (U.S.) — Drama.
I. Berkove, Lawrence I.
II. Scharnhorst, Gary.
III. Davis, Sam P. (Sam Post), 1850–1918. Prince of Timbuctoo. IV. Title.
    PS1827.L83 2006
    812'.408—dc22

                            2005032834

DESIGN AND COMPOSTION: *Mina Yamashita*

To Gail and Sandy

Contents

Introduction / 1

PART ONE: *The Luck of Roaring Camp,* by Bret Harte / 7
    Introduction / 9
    The Luck of Roaring Camp
        in One Prologue and Two Acts
        by Bret Harte and M. de Seigneur / 22

PART TWO: *The Prince of Timbuctoo,* by Sam Davis / 129
    Introduction / 131
    The Prince of Timbuctoo:
        A Comic Opera in Three Acts
        Libretto by Sam P. Davis / 145

Index / 225

Introduction

Despite the canon reformation of the past generation, our understanding of nineteenth- and early twentieth-century American literature is far from complete. Dramatic literature from the period is largely ignored, for example, and the literature of the American West is still scanted. Henry James, W. D. Howells, Mark Twain, and Bret Harte together wrote some sixty plays, most of them long forgotten. Put another way, Harte may be a semi-canonical author, but he is known for only a fraction of his writings. Sam Davis is almost completely unknown, unjustly so in our estimation. This edition of lost plays by both western authors will attempt to redress this neglect and make the case for renewed attention to them on the bases of literary history and literary merit.

Surprisingly, perhaps, the trans-Mississippi West was a center of theatrical activity from the earliest days of white settlement. Theater was thriving in St. Louis as early as 1820,[1] and once gold and silver were discovered in California and Nevada, even before mining camps metamorphosed into towns and cities, theater was one of the major entertainments in that region, too. Self-respecting small communities considered it de rigueur to have—in addition to schools, churches, and a newspaper or two—at least one opera hall. Larger communities required more than one. Virginia City in the 1870s, for example, with a permanent population of about twenty-five thousand and a floating population of another five to ten thousand, was the main city of Nevada's Comstock Lode. It boasted a theater, two opera halls, several music halls, and a National Guard hall. For most of the decade it had the largest population of any American city between Chicago and San Francisco and it was a routine stop on national theatrical tours. The theaters usually hosted a lecture, play, or musical performance every evening, plus an interlude or a short farce, olio, or dramatic reading. When performances were particularly popular, matinees were scheduled on weekends. Major theatrical troupes and famous personalities from the East—and also from Europe—regularly toured California and the Comstock because the western mining regions paid well. Drama also paid well, so writers with a national or even international reputation wrote for the theater and often adapted their fiction to it. In the literary market of the Gilded Age, writing a successful play was vastly more profitable than selling novels and stories to the magazines. As Harte once explained to his wife, "A good play ought to give me certainly $3,000 a year for a year or two."[2] Little wonder that lesser-known authors, including Sam Davis, also tried their hands at playwriting.

More particularly, they tried their hands at plays using themes and characters from the American West. These were undeniably popular topics for the legitimate theater in the late-nineteenth century and most of the best-known playwrights in the country predictably tried to tap the market. Stuart Hyde estimates that some 1,200 plays about the frontier were written between 1849 and 1917.[3] Among the western melodramas staged in New York and Boston during the period were James J. McCloskey's *Across the Continent* (1870), Augustin Daly's *Horizon* (1871), Joaquin Miller's *First Families of the Sierras* (1875), Bartley Campbell's *My Partner* (1879), Augustus Thomas's *In Mizzoura* (1893), Clyde Fitch's *The Cowboy and the Lady* (1899), a theatrical version of Owen Wister's *The Virginian* (1904), David Belasco's *The Girl of the Golden West* (1905), and William Vaughn Moody's *The Great Divide* (1906). Such plays were exciting spectacles on stage, featuring live horses and frequent gunplay, and such exotic types as redshirt miners, primitive Indians, inscrutable Chinese laundrymen, and decayed Spanish aristocrats. The West was even more sensationalized on the "illegitimate" stage in such productions as Frank Mayo's *Davy Crockett* (1873) and Ned Buntline's *The Scouts of the Plains* (1872), which featured no less a showman than Buffalo Bill Cody. Later the impresario of his Wild West show, Cody performed in at least one new stage play per year between 1875 and 1882.[4]

Western drama did more than merely exploit interregional differences between East and West. From the earliest years of the Republic, American writers explored the so-called international theme, dramatizing the encounters between inhabitants of the New World and the Old. Royall Tyler's popular play *The Contrast* (1787) pitted American moral probity and innocence against the scheming immorality of an English scoundrel—and American virtue triumphed. It continued to triumph for the next century and beyond, but by the middle of the nineteenth century some American authors began to offer variations on the theme. As early as 1869, Mark Twain satirized the formula in *The Innocents Abroad*. Twain's book also reflected his embrace of the values of the West, especially its skepticism about appearances and its rejection of glib stereotypes. The western slope was not an isolated region a continent away. On the contrary, authors who wrote for its mining camps and towns had a shrewd grasp of human nature, in both its varnished and unvarnished forms. They were familiar with many nationalities and, while inclined to be patriotic, were under no illusions that all Americans were innocent and all continentals were decadent. The two plays in this collection, in their depiction of the clash of Old and New World cultures, are additional examples of the unexpected erudition of western authors at the time.

There was a historical context for this clash. Many works on the international theme (e.g., Charles Dickens's *American Notes* and *David Copperfield,* Frances Trollope's *Domestic Manners of the Americans,* Henry James's *The Europeans,* and Edith Wharton's *The Age of Innocence*) feature European visitors to the United

States. Early in the nineteenth century relatively few narratives by native writers featured Americans abroad, and those that did (e.g., Washington Irving's *The Sketch Book*) were often tailored for the European literary market. After all, Americans who went to Europe at the time were a rare breed. Only privileged families were able to send their sons and daughters abroad for a *Wanderjahr*, for the Grand Tour, for study in the schools, or for "finishing." With the advent of steam power and the rise of tourism after the Civil War, however, middle-class Americans for the first time were able to afford extended European travel. Passengers departing by steamer from the four major Atlantic ports for Europe increased from about twenty thousand in 1860 to over eighty thousand in 1890 and to over a hundred thousand in 1900.[5] During the final decades of the century more than ever before American writers were enjoined to explore this new cross-cultural experience.

The two plays in this collection portray Americans afoot in the Old World like several of the "boys" in Twain's *The Innocents Abroad* and Christopher Newman, the "great American Barbarian" from California, in James's *The American* (1877). Other well-known fictional Americans affected by their European experiences include James's protagonists in "Daisy Miller" (1878), *The Portrait of a Lady* (1881), *The Ambassadors* (1903), and *The Golden Bowl* (1904); and Countess Olenska, née Ellen Mingott, in Edith Wharton's *The Age of Innocence* (1920). While James and Wharton, both raised in the genteel tradition of the East, famously depicted Americans from the educated and cultured classes, Twain, Harte, and Davis, shaped by the rough and tumble of the West, were inclined to a thoughtful sophistication grounded in practical experience that played a part in distinguishing them from their more genteel contemporaries. They chose their protagonists from the upwardly mobile working classes. The differences are telling. The novels in the genteel tradition typically depict the timid or tepid response of monied Americans to the refined culture of the continent. The more middlebrow works portray the reactions of working- and middle-class Americans to the appeals of Old World wealth or to its audacious claims of superiority.

More to the point: both plays in this volume address the phenomenon of female American protagonists, one an ingénue and the other an adventuress, who are, in effect, offered the chance to gain aristocratic titles by marrying into noble Old World families. As early as the 1880s, American newspapers listed such marriages and occasionally gloated in their failures.[6] On the one hand, James and Wharton underscored the tragic consequences of such asymmetrical unions; on the other, Harte in particular contrasted the decadence of artificial European aristocrats who sell their birthright for a pottage with the talent and virtue of natural American aristocrats who earn their rank and so level the matrimonial playing field. Thus, in his comedy, Harte portrayed the ultimate triumph of democratic values over social privilege. Davis similarly glimpsed a brighter future by imagining individuals who transcend accidents of social, national, and racial difference. The protagonists in his play begin as mercenary opportunists from a shockingly cynical America, but once Orndorff and Dooley are enlisted on the side of true love, Orndorff at least is willing to settle for a good life in Timbuctoo.

Both Harte and Davis sought to resolve the melodramatic plots of these plays with neat and happy endings. Had the two of them been resolutely cheery in all their works, these particular scripts might easily be prosecuted for the crime of adhering to predictable narrative formulas. But Harte was famous for his unwillingness to pander to public opinion — his tales often contained tragic overtones and he sometimes deliberately wrote to provoke or offend — and on his part Davis was deeply concerned with ethical issues.[7] The typical plots of these authors were neither as straightforward as a fraudulent stock dividend nor as simple as an uncontested election.

Harte and Davis were optimists, but they were not blind optimists. Still, they believed the example of America and the character of Americans would change the Old World for the better. In the final analysis their faith in the leveling influence of the American West is a powerful legacy.

—Lawrence I. Berkove
University of Michigan—Dearborn

—Gary Scharnhorst
University of New Mexico

Notes

1. William G. B. Carson, *The Theatre on the Frontier: The Early Years of the St. Louis Stage* (Chicago: University of Chicago Press, 1932), passim.

2. Gary Scharnhorst, ed., *Selected Letters of Bret Harte* (Norman and London: University of Oklahoma Press, 1997), 314.

3. Cited in Roger Hall, *Performing the American Frontier, 1870–1906* (New York: Cambridge University Press, 2001), 4.

4. Ibid., 62.

5. Christof Wegelin, "The Rise of the International Novel," *PMLA* 77 (1962): 307.

6. For example, "Titled Girls/New York Furnishes the Largest and Most Notable List/The American Craze/Purchasing Alliances With Nobility—Brides With Splendor and Misery," *San Francisco Examiner*, 15 April 1888, p. 13. This article was probably reprinted as an exchange item from an eastern newspaper.

7. See Lawrence I. Berkove, "Samuel Post Davis," in *Dictionary of Literary Biography: Nineteenth-Century American Fiction Writers*, ed. Kent P. Ljungquist (Detroit: Gale, 1999), 92–99.

PART ONE

The Luck of Roaring Camp

by Bret Harte

Introduction

Like many another American writers of the late nineteenth century, including his friends Henry James and W. D. Howells, Bret Harte longed to write commercially successful plays. In 1870, even before he left California to test his literary fortunes in the East, he agreed to write a script for the actor Lawrence Barrett featuring some of the characters he had popularized in his stories for the *Overland Monthly*. Like most of his endeavors at the time, however, the script was never produced, probably not even completed. Two years later, Harte contracted with the producer Augustin Daly to script a five-act play suitable for the Fifth Avenue Theatre in New York. He was to be paid a royalty of a hundred dollars per performance or six hundred dollars per week with a thousand dollar advance to be paid upon delivery of a suitable manuscript.[1] Again, the play was supposed to feature some of the characters in Harte's *Overland* stories. He even persuaded the dramatist Dion Boucicault to help him write the melodrama, entitled *Kentuck*, and reports of their collaboration were leaked to the press. The *New York Tribune* welcomed the news: "The skill and dexterity of Mr. Boucicault in dramatic construction, his mastery of all scenic resources, combined with that delicate insight and power of characterization which Mr. Harte possesses in such an extraordinary degree, offer a guarantee of a great success."[2] Isn't it pretty to think so? In fact, their collaboration was hardly a propitious one. Boucicault soon complained to Daly that "Harte is very dilatory and erratic" yet "very anxious to get the work done." He "thinks we can scurry over the ground more rapidly than is consistent with safety."[3] Predictably, Boucicault and Harte apparently failed to finish the script of *Kentuck*; certainly it was never produced.

To be sure, over the years three of Harte's plays were produced on Broadway—*Two Men of Sandy Bar* in 1876; *Ah Sin*, written in collaboration with Mark Twain, in 1877; and *Sue*, written in collaboration with T. Edgar Pemberton, in 1898. None of them was a marked success, however. *Two Men of Sandy Bar* was a baggy monster, requiring in its original version some four hours to perform. The drama critic for the *New York Times* called it "the worst failure witnessed on the boards of our theatres for years" and "the most dismal mass of trash that was ever put into dramatic shape before a New York audience." It was less a script than a "nondescript."[4] Similarly, *Ah Sin* was perhaps the most disastrous collaboration in the history of American letters. It lost money during the six months it kept the boards, and even Twain was forced to concede that it was "a most abject & incurable failure."[5] Thanks to the acting of Annie Russell in the title role, *Sue* earned modest royalties for Harte and Pemberton during its runs in London and New York at the close of the nineteenth century, though the play has not been performed now for over a hundred years. Still, such mixed success did not entirely discourage Harte from writing plays. In all, he wrote, usually with collaborators, a total of eleven of them. To date, the scripts of only *Two Men*, *Ah Sin*, and *Sue* have been known to survive. Harte published *Two Men* in 1877; a script of *Ah Sin* was discovered among Daly's papers and published in 1961; and Pemberton published *Sue* in 1902, the same year as Harte's death.

Until now, that is. The unpublished script of *The Luck of Roaring Camp*, loosely based upon Harte's story first published in the *Overland Monthly* for July 1868 and long known to be among his "lost" plays, fortunately survives among the Harte Papers in the Library of Congress. Fortunately, the vexed history of the script can be reconstructed from Harte's letters and diary. Harte began to write the play in June 1882 in collaboration with his friend, hostess, and occasional amanuensis Mme Van de Velde, the wife of the chancellor of the Belgian Legation in London. Van de Velde, who signed her contribution to the play *M. de Seigneur* (or Monsieur Lord), was a talented writer in her own right—her play *As in a Looking Glass* would be performed by Sarah Bernhardt to laudatory reviews in London and Paris a few years later. In any event, as Harte wrote his wife Anna in July 1882, "I am determined to succeed with a play this season, and at Boucicault's suggestion I have begun to dramatize 'The Luck of Roaring Camp.' I have read him the first act and he gives me the greatest encouragement."[6]

The collaborators pegged away at the project during their vacation in Bournemouth that summer and they had completed a draft of it by early September 1882. During a visit with his friends John Hay and Clarence King in London that month, as Howells later wrote to Mark Twain, they heard Harte "read a comedy he has been colaborating [sic] with a Belgian lady. He has turned the 'Luck' of Roaring Camp into a girl, and brought her to Paris, with all his Californians where she has adventures."[7] Hay at least enjoyed the performance. He wrote Harte from Paris the following December to inquire when the play was to be performed and to promise to come to London to see it "if I have strength enough to lie in a gutter and call for a coach."[8] Unfortunately, Harte's theatrical patron was less impressed than was Hay. As Harte reported to Anna in late September,

> I've just finished two months work on the 'Luck,' and am somewhat disappointed to find from Boucicault, on submitting it to him, that the two last acts are radically wrong in structure—in other words, I must *begin it all over again*. You know how hard it is for me to write a play; imagine how provoked and exasperated I feel at having lost my holiday in such ungracious work only to find it futile. Of course, I shall not give it up—but it means that I must turn my leisure now

to writing some little story *for money* to keep the pot boiling before I can go on with the larger work which is to pay me better in the end. I am haunted by the recollection that the time I have lost might have been worth so much to me in story-writings. It seems I can write dialogue like an angel, draw characters like a heaven born genius, but I can't make *situations* and *plots*.[9]

Undeterred, Harte next tried to interest Augustin Daly in a précis of the script. "I have finished a play in three acts called 'The Luck of Roaring Camp,'" he wrote to Daly:

The first act—or prologue as it really is—is an almost literal dramatization of my original story, except that the child is a girl instead of a boy. The two remaining acts, which take place in Paris, where the girl, grown a young lady, has been placed at school by her rough but devoted fathers of Roaring Camp, is of course a new conception. It is a comedy, naturally—the humorous situations dominate, but the rough element is never low comedy—nor is it ever obstrusive or protracted. All my old characters appear:— Oakhurst, Stumpy, Kentuck, and Skaggs. The principal is, of course, the heroine—a kind of intelligent "fille du Regiment," a sort of boyish ingénue—such as Chaumont of the *Varieties* or Samary of the *Français* would play in Paris now. I don't know what actresses you have "to the fore" in New York; there are half a dozen I remember who could do it nicely. If Lotta [Crabtree] would repress herself a little she might.[10]

This overture came to naught apparently because, as Harte wrote later, the English managers were "more or less afraid to risk it with

English actors and English audiences."[11] Anna Harte also expressed reservations about the dramatization on the grounds that it omitted the "poetic element" of the original tale. Harte conceded the force of her objection but insisted that his old story "is only used as a prologue to the play of the other acts, where 'The Luck' is a girl who has been sent to Paris and is educated by the wealthy members of the old Camp, who visit her occasionally. It is in this mingling and contact of these rough men with this high-super-civilized Old World and the love for their adopted daughter, 'The Luck,' that I hope to get dramatic as well as humorous effect. 'The Luck' is called 'Fortuna del Campo Clamoroso' (which is good Spanish as well as Italian) to the great mystification of the *noblesse* with historic names."[12] Harte was so confident the play would make money he copyrighted it in England in Mme Van de Velde's name so that his creditors back in the States could not garnish his income from it.

He need not have gone to such trouble. After he completed his revisions of the script in February 1883, Boucicault turned it down again. Harte asked his friend and agent Charles Watrous to send it to Charles Frohman (1860–1915), manager of the Madison Square Theatre in New York, who agreed in July to stage it the following spring, contingent on making his own revisions and alterations in the script. Frohman initially offered Harte ten dollars per performance, then fifteen dollars, to a maximum of ten thousand dollars so long as the play kept the stage. On his part, Harte rightly suspected Frohman's offer was merely a ruse to acquire dramatic rights to his story, its title, and his name and then to resell them to a third party, and he testily refused the terms. The offer was "ridiculously low," as he wrote his son Frank, and "I have declined to take the responsibility of his alterations without seeing them."[13] Instead, Harte asked Frohman for twenty-five dollars per performance and a forfeiture fee of five hundred dollars if the play was "not acted in a twelvemonth."[14] "My terms are based upon the advice of good business men here—managers both in England and America—as well as my own judgement," he explained to Anna. Among them, "Bronson Howard, one of the Madison Square Theatre dramatists," who lived at the time in St. John's Wood in London and "who is an acquaintance of mine, advises me that Frohman's offer is too low."[15] An entire year after completing a draft of the play, with the script still an orphan, Harte belatedly realized it was likely to remain unpublished and unproduced. As he admitted to his wife, "I fear the play will not amount to much in America—here it is at present unmarketable."[16] Boucicault eventually offered roughly the same deal as did Frohman, though Harte also declined it because he considered Boucicault an incompetent businessman: "I doubt Boucicault's *means and ability* to run the play as well as Frohman." In the end, he finally settled with Frohman for fifteen dollars per performance, ceasing at ten thousand dollars.[17] Inasmuch as his script was "to be altered and revised" he tentatively planned to return to the United States for the first time in nearly fifteen years so that he might "possibly oversee one or two rehearsals."[18]

Unfortunately, Frohman never staged the play. In June 1884, when Harte had expected *The Luck of Roaring Camp* to be in rehearsal, Frohman sailed to London "with the MS of my Play and the unpleasant information that it must be almost entirely rearranged and rewritten before it can appear," as he wrote to Anna. "This was the play that I expected would be paying me a royalty this autumn! The work must be done at once—it will take the better part of two months to complete."[19] Harte was eventually paid a small forfeiture fee by Frohman[20]—which in turn went to pay some of his old debts in New York.

Harte refused to shelve the project. He next approached the theatrical impresario David Belasco about staging the play in New York. Belasco rose to the bait and, in June 1885, he proposed to rewrite and supervise the production of the play in New York, paying Harte an advance of five hundred dollars and one-third of all royalties on it,[21] though again nothing came of the proposal. The comic actor and theatrical manager John L. Toole offered to stage the play, "that long-travailing infant," in 1886, but Harte withdrew the script when he decided that "either the pathetic or the farcical" element in the play "must be dominant; that I could not blend them, and that either Toole or the audience must be disappointed."[22] He reluctantly concluded that the play failed to maintain a consistent tone, and he abandoned the attempt to find a producer for it. Finally, in 1890, after protracted negotiations, Harte authorized Boucicault to dramatize the story—in effect, he sold dramatic rights to the title and characters for fifteen pounds per week so long as the play remained in production. Boucicault began to write the adaptation, which incorporated no material from the script Harte had written with Mme Van de Velde, but died before it was completed—yet another unfortunate turn of the screw to Harte's financial fate. The surviving fragment—the first act of a projected three-act play—was briefly staged as a curtain raiser by Frohman at the Empire Theatre in New York in May 1894. Despite his contract, Harte received no royalties from the production because Boucicault's supposed collaborator claimed he had done all the writing. "It's a miserable affair," as he complained to Anna, "and a mixture of *deceit* and downright swindling and robbery, which I am unfortunately accustomed to in my dealings with my countrymen ever since I left America."[23] In all, the several plays based on Harte's stories in the late nineteenth and early twentieth centuries, among them *Gabriel Conroy*, *M'liss*, *Salomy Jane*, and *The Luck of Roaring Camp*, paid huge dividends to many actors and theatrical producers at the time—but earned Harte hardly anything at all.

Still, despite his struggles to succeed as a playwright, Harte's influence on the formula western, particularly as it developed in western movies, can hardly be overstated. Between 1909 and 1955 no fewer than twenty-four feature films starring such actors as Douglas

Fairbanks, Ronald Reagan, and Mary Pickford were explicitly based on Harte's fiction. Such Hollywood classics as *Stagecoach* (1939) featured an ensemble cast drawn from Harte's original stable of character-types, among them the chivalrous outlaw, the gallant gambler, the crusty stagecoach driver, the whore with a heart of gold, the drunken doctor, the cowardly dude, and the eastern vestal of civilization. In *High Noon* (1952), Grace Kelly played a lineal descendant of the schoolmarm Harte introduced in *The Idyl of Red Gulch*. Walter Brennan played a character literally named Stumpy, one of Harte's redshirt miners, in *Rio Bravo* (1959), directed by Howard Hawks. The character of the irreverent gambler Bret [*sic*] Maverick, played by James Garner in the popular '50s television series, was obviously inspired by Harte's Jack Hamlin and John Oakhurst. Put another way, Harte's script of *The Luck of Roaring Camp* is a snapshot in the early evolution of the "performed western."

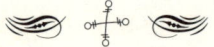

Despite his claim that the play "is an almost literal dramatization of my original story, except that the child is a girl instead of a boy," Harte and Mme Van de Velde freely adapted his original story for dramatic purposes. Never very skilled in the techniques of playwriting, Harte depended upon such tired and tested plot devices as mistaken identities and chance reunions to structure the farce, a precursor of the "screwball comedies" of the 1930s. The collaborators were also careful to maintain standards of middle-class propriety in their revision of the original story. For example, whereas in the original tale Cherokee Sal, the mother of "the Luck," is obviously a camp whore, in the dramatic version she arrives in Roaring Camp only three days before giving birth to the child after she is thrown out of a "sneaking settlement" downriver. Cherokee Sal is also described by Stumpy in the play "as white as the snow on them peaks"—thus Harte and Mme Van de Velde evaded the nettlesome issue of miscegenation in acts 1 and 2. That is, whereas in Harte's original story "the Luck" is described as "an Injun baby," in the play Fortuna's native lineage is almost completely ignored, apparently so that the role might be played by a fair-complexioned actress in the tradition of the melodramatic ingénue. Because the playwrights changed the sex of the protagonist from male to female, moreover, they were obliged to invent the character of Mrs. Stumpy to care for the growing girl. They also tamed or chastened the vulgar dialogue of the original story (e.g., "d—d little cuss" in the story becomes "darned little cuss" in the play).[24] And the child does not die in the play, as he does at the end of Harte's original story.

More to the point, this dramatic version of "The Luck of Roaring Camp" exhibits Harte's belief in the social solvent of interclass marriage. The playwrights affirm that even a child with the undistinguished background of Fortuna—born illegitimately and raised in the mining fields—is yet able to muster the graces of cultured society. Though she speaks in vernacular dialect, drinks liquor, gambles, flirts, parries inquiries into her parentage, "rides without a groom, swims, talks loud, laughs till the tears run down her cheeks," Fortuna is simply an all-American girl whose democratic tastes do not evaporate in the glare of social privilege. "You wanted to tame my little girl," Oakhurst observes. "Marriage will soon do that." To the end of the play Fortuna remains staunchly loyal—"true as steel, pure as gold"—to her rustic "Fathers" and to the déclassé Mrs. Stumpy. "Did you think I was ashamed of the homeliest of them all [Kentuck]," she plaintively asks Mme Joubard, the Marquise, and Paul, "and that I am not proud of being their child, ah yes, far more proud than you can ever be of your birth, your titles, and your rank?" She importunely loses half her fortune, but she does not change, nor does Paul's love for her falter. She chooses to marry Paul despite his poverty. (To be sure, after the couple reunites in act 2, Fortuna regains her wealth.) In brief, neither Fortuna nor Paul betrays the least hint of class consciousness (though Oakhurst does claim rather cynically that Paul wants "to marry a young girl" like Fortuna "who defies" the "rigid school of continental propriety" in which he was raised). Harte thus implies a saving grace in some of the aristocrats, a recognition that character may transcend class or class differences. The Baron and Mme Joubard lack this virtue, but Paul, his mother, and "French Pete" Joubard have nurtured it. In brief, Harte seems to commend American democracy for fostering respect for the lower classes even among the enlightened aristocracy. He believed Europe was changing for the better under the influence of the egalitarian example set by America. Though often faulted for his sentimentality, Harte was to his credit genuinely optimistic about the prospects for social progress and democratic reform, as the play suggests.

On the other hand, he also depicted how some members of the aristocracy resisted social progress and democratization. Harte often privately berated Americans for their mindless worship of European aristocracy. As he wrote his wife in July 1885, "I really believe that the American reverence for the aristocracy and their habits is greater than it is among those to the manner born."[25] His adaptation of "The Luck" becomes nothing less than a satire of aristocratic pretensions, at least those harbored by such fops and snobs as the fortune-hunting Baron de Trempes (whose very surname means "calibre" in French) and Madame Joubard. These two characters are faintly reminiscent of such Parisian aristocrats as the provincial Bellegarde family in Henry James's novel *The American* (1877), written only a few years before Harte's play. Similarly, Fortuna's friend Antoinette not only is acutely proud of her class privilege but is anxious to improve her social rank through marriage. (Ironically, French Pete had proposed naming the infant Fortuna "Antoinette" in the prologue; that is, Harte implies that under different circumstances "the Luck" might have grown up to be as snooty and vapid as her foil.) And while such former miners as Oakhurst and Boston escape the working class to become distinguished diplomats and bankers (courtesy of the gold discovered in Roaring Camp), Skaggs and Stumpy with their malapropisms are mere caricatures, precursors to the farcical comedians Bud Abbott and Lou Costello. In the end, the social solvent of marriage cannot dissolve all class barriers in Harte's melodrama any more than in life.

To be sure, the theatrical adaptation of "The Luck of Roaring Camp" Harte composed with Mme Van de Velde is a small nugget or pocket of "color," not a rich vein of gold ore that invites a large-scale mining operation. Much like *Ah Sin*, however, *The Luck* is a literary curio fit for display among the other relics of western American literary history. The script retains a charm acknowledged by virtually everyone who read it in the mid-1880s, among them many of the most prominent writers, actors, and theatrical producers of the age.

The manuscript of *The Luck of Roaring Camp* was donated to the Library of Congress in 1952 by the heirs of Charles Watrous, to whom Harte had entrusted it some seventy years before, hoping to find a producer for the play in the United States. The prologue and first act are in Harte's handwriting, the second act in Mme Van de Velde's. I am also indebted to my friend and colleague Bob Gish for his help in deciphering parts of the manuscript.

Notes

1. Joseph F. Daly, *The Life of Augustin Daly* (New York: Macmillan, 1947), 171; Marvin Felheim, *The Theater of Augustin Daly* (Cambridge: Harvard University Press, 1956), 296.

2. "Personal," *New York Tribune*, 29 August 1876, 5:1.

3. Daly, *The Life of Augustin Daly*, 173–74.

4. "Amusements," *New York Times*, 29 August 1876, 5:4–5.

5. Henry Nash Smith and William M. Gibson, eds., *Mark Twain–Howells Letters*, 2 vols. (Cambridge: Belknap, 1960), 1:206.

6. Geoffrey Bret Harte, ed., *The Letters of Bret Harte* (Boston and New York: Houghton Mifflin, 1926), 210.

7. Smith and Gibson, *Mark Twain–Howells Letters*, 1:416.

8. Quoted in Gary Scharnhorst, *Bret Harte: Opening the American Literary West* (Norman and London: University of Oklahoma Press, 2000), 172.

9. Harte, *The Letters of Bret Harte*, 213.

10. Daly, *The Life of Augustin Daly*, 362–63. Harte had known the actress Lotta Crabtree (1847–1924) in California some fifteen years before.

11. Quoted in Scharnhorst, *Bret Harte* (New York: Twayne, 1992), 87.

12. Harte, *The Letters of Bret Harte*, 218.

13. Bradford A. Booth, "Unpublished Letters of Bret Harte," *American Literature* 16 (May 1944): 136–37.

14. Gary Scharnhorst ed., *Selected Letters of Bret Harte* (Norman and London: University of Oklahoma Press, 1997), 299.

15. Ibid., 296–97.

16. Harte, *The Letters of Bret Harte*, 239.

17. Bret Harte to Anna Harte, 15 October 1883 (Alderman Library, University of Virginia).

18. Scharnhorst, *Selected Letters*, 304.

19. Ibid., 314.

20. Harte, *The Letters of Bret Harte*, 269.

21. David Belasco to Bret Harte, 3 June 1885 (John Bret-Harte).

22. Harte, *The Letters of Bret Harte*, 296.

23. Scharnhorst, *Bret Harte*, 203.

24. This change in the dialogue of the original story was, in effect, Harte's concession to popular taste. He had to defend himself against accusations of obscenity when the story was first published in 1868 partly because the miners "swear."

25. Scharnhorst, *Selected Letters*, 327.

The Luck of Roaring Camp
in One Prologue and Two Acts
by Bret Harte and M. de Seigneur

Characters in Prologue
Original Members of Roaring Camp
Jack Oakhurst
Boston
Stumpy
Kentuck
Dublin Bay
Dungaree Jack
Sydney Duck
Miners
Mrs. Smith   Wife of Stumpy
A Baby

Locality
Roaring Camp, Calaveras County, California

Time
1852

Prologue

Roaring Camp. A Cañon, rocks, pine trees, water fall, camp fires on Left. Stumpy's Cabin disclosing interior when door is open. Distant view of snow capped Sierra. Kentuck, Stumpy, Boston, Dublin Bay, French Pete and miners in rough working picturesque costumes discovered in groups, smoking, drinking, card playing.

Oakhurst centre beside barrel: Order, gentlemen! *French Pete, Stumpy and Kentuck turn quick towards Oakhurst half rising. Boston, Dublin Bay, Skaggs and other miners continue their occupations without heeding.*
Oakhurst: Order! *French Pete, Stumpy and Kentuck try to enlist attention of others, but vainly. After a pause Oakhurst draws pistol and fires it in the air. All spring to their feet, grasping rifles and revolvers, and turn excitedly toward Oakhurst.*
Oakhurst quietly returning the pistol to pocket: I said Order! Gentlemen! *All slowly resume their places with faces turned toward Oakhurst.*
Skaggs—regretfully: It wasn't a free fight after all.
Oakhurst: It has been the custom of this camp, gentlemen, to call a meeting to discuss any matter involving the common interests of its members. A circumstance has just occurred which concerns not only the present, but the future of Roaring Camp. *Cries of Hear! Hear!* Three days ago a strange woman arrived here in this camp in a fainting condition, and died in giving birth to a child. Death has perhaps been frequent here, owing to the liberality of our institutions, but I believe this is the first record of a birth in it. I call this meeting to know what steps shall be taken in this matter.

French Pete (with foreign accent): I move that Mr. John Oakhurst take the chair.

Kentuck: I second the motion.

Oakhurst: It is moved and seconded that the speaker take the chair. Those who are in favour of that motion please say Aye.

All except Boston: Aye!

Oakhurst: Those to the contrary No.

Boston: No. *All start. Some gather angrily around Boston. Business. Skaggs is seen expostulating.*

Oakhurst: The Ayes have it. *Significantly.* When this meeting has adjourned, the Chairman will remain to receive an explanation from the "nos."

Boston attempting to rise but held down by Skaggs and others: But! I'll give it right here. I rise to a question of principle. By the laws of the community no woman of the female persuasion is allowed to find shelter in Roaring Camp. The rule excluding women is written in the Constitution. *Cries of "Hear, hear!"* It is an iron rule. Self preservation is the first law of nature.

Stumpy: The gentleman from Red Dog reports that the woman is dead, and no longer subject to debate.

Oakhurst: I take a note of the objection.

All: Order! Order!

Skaggs interposing: One moment boys. The gentlemen from Red Dog allows he meant no offence to the chair, but the fact being that the chair bet him seventy dollars yesterday that this same baby would stay in this camp as long as *he* would, it looks to him as if the odds were agin him, if Mr. Oakhurst has the chair. It's a question of privilege, that's all gentlemen.

French Pete to Oakhurst with slight French accent: Perhaps it might be a leetle more parliamentary if the honourable Chair would decide that . . .

Oakhurst: The bet's off. And, gentlemen, we will proceed to business.

French Pete: I move that our distinguished fellow citizen Mr. Stumpy, who has resolved himself out the Committee of the whole in charge of the Bebe, be invited to address the meeting.

All: Stumpy! Stumpy!

Oakhurst: Order! *Pause.* It is moved and seconded that Mr. Stumpy address the meeting. *Stumpy who has been endeavoring to slip away is dragged forward and placed beside Oakhurst. He laboriously shakes hands with everybody and wipes his face with his handkerchief. He is half bashful, half self important, always serious. Business.*

Stumpy hesitatingly at first: It ain't mor'n than three days ago, boys, a stranger, an unbeknownst woman—Cherokee Sal by name, waltzes down yer, into this camp, and drops down just here—in front of my shanty, all in a heap and fainted dead away. She was as white as the snow on them peaks and had about as much life about her. Mebbee I'm wrong, mebbee I'm lying! But I leave it to you all, boys, *appealing to the crowd,* if it wasn't—*cries of "aye," "aye" and "go on."* Well! I picked up that forlorn critter and packs her on my back into that yer shanty, and she lies there twixt life and death for three days. The chances were about ten to one, and I leave it to you boys, if there weren't bets on it, and money changed hands in this yer camp the night she died. Why, Skaggs there bet a cool twenty on her living, and there not being any baby at all.

Skaggs embarrassedly: Dry up on that.

Stumpy: Nat'rally he lost, for that poor critter died and a baby was born. It wasn't a big one, but it was a baby for all that, and it's alive and adoing well in that shanty. And now boys, mebbee you want to know how that there baby managed to keep steps with the music of this yer camp, and not a woman or a cow inside o' fifty miles. Well boys, you know Jinny, my donkey, her that totes gravel from my claim, though I do say it, there ain't a brighter, nor a cuter, nor a softer hearted donkey goin'—and—and—boys, she's a mother herself. *Cries of "three cheers for Jinny" and laughter.*

Oakhurst: Order, gentlemen!

Boston: I move that in the absence of Jinny Mr. Stumpy's report be accepted as hers also. *Cries of "Silence" and "Order."*

Boston fiercely: I *am* in order. Let the matter end here. We have determined to give the woman a decent burial—a darned sight better than she deserved—and no thanks, gentlemen, to that sneaking settlement down on the river that must have turned her out and let her drift right into Roaring Camp to die. Are we expected to take the tailings[1] they wash down from their sluice boxes,[2] and they keep the gold? No gentlemen, I move that a committee be formed to find out where she came from, and then send her kid down there by express, marked C.O.D.

Skaggs: And then waltz down there ourselves, and clean them out for their impudence.

Dublin Bay: And teach their dirty souls that the next time they send an innocent baby to Roaring Camp to be born there, they'll first give the mother a decent burial themselves. *Cries of "Order!" and confusion.*

French Pete: We are not here, comrades, to cast stones at the woman[3] whose grave we shall dig on that hill side. Whatever she *was*, must be buried with her there. All that shall live of her now will be her child, and the leetle flowers that grow above her grave. If it is proposed now to tear them clean up by the roots they have put down in Roaring Camp, why good! then some of the men who have made Roaring Camp what it is, *will* know the reason why.

Boston his hand on revolver: Is that meant for me, French Pete?

French Pete: Well! I did not take quite your measure, but for a ready made article, it does not fit you bad. *Confusion and cries of "Order," "Sit down." Oakhurst trifling with pistol. The gentleman from Red Dog is reminded that he is not in order — but he is . . . in range.*

Skaggs: Mr. Chairman, I reckon I can square the difference between the gentleman from Red Dog, and the Frenchman from Sacramento. Here we are, so to speak, making our own game in Roaring Camp. Here comes a stranger, a woman, to take a hand in it. Well, she leaves the board before the game's played out. What happens? Why not rally according to the rules, she forfeits what she has put in the pot, her baby — and that belongs to all who have a hand in Roaring Camp.

Dublin Bay: Bedad! It's spaking ye are now.

Skaggs: Share and share alike.

All: Share and share alike.

Kentuck: I move, Mr. Chairman, afore we settle this matter, this yer meeting adjourn to take a look at the property. We've had a report from Mr. Stumpy, but we ain't had no exhibition of the assets.

Skaggs: I second the motion. *Stumpy exhibits great agitation and endeavours to appeal to Oakhurst in dumb show. Business.*

Oakhurst unheeding him: It is moved and seconded that this meeting now adjourn to personally inspect the property bequeathed to it. You in favour of the motion will say "Aye."

All except Stumpy: Aye!

Oakhurst leaving chair and taking Stumpy aside: Not a word. It is for the best. Let them see the child while they care to. Leave the rest to me.

Stumpy appealingly: But say a word for her, John!

Oakhurst smiling: I say a word. That baby's a sermon, and a stump speech in one. Go! *Exit Stumpy in hut.* To avoid crowding, gentlemen, we'll enter the cabin on the right, single file and pass out on the left. Those who wish to contribute anything for the orphan will find a hat handy. *All retire left wing and reappear in file. Oakhurst takes position leaning beside door. Right with folded arms. French Pete takes similar attitude. Left with a hat in his hand for contributions.*

Oakhurst in a low voice: Ready! *First miner steps forward laughing and embarrassed—pauses in front of door, looks in, then at Oakhurst, takes off his hat (men applauding the act of courtesy) and enters. After a moment reappears from door left, serious and thoughtful. French Pete offers hat, miner starts, recovers himself, fumbles anxiously in his pocket, and drops some loose silver in the hat. Pauses, reflects, tears open his shirt, and takes from his neck a cheap locket, drops it in the hat and goes slowly to wings. Same business for each man, modified as to character.*

French Pete with assumed impressiveness: Flynn of Virginia—two dollars and thirty-seven cents cash and a silver locket. *Miner pulls out note book and makes entries of donations.—Enter second miner—business as before.*

French Pete: Sydney Duck[4] of Australia. Fifteen dollars, a Bank of England note for five pounds, and a silver spoon. The initials not the giver's. *Enter Dublin Bay—same business.* Dublin Bay of the same, twenty-five cents in silver, a tobacco box silver. A Father Mathew temperance medal,[5] silver, a lever watch plated.

Dublin Bay: Faith! Is it real gold I'd be wearing in such company.

French Pete—continues: Enter Boston. Boston, Twenty dollars, a silver mounted revolver—Euclid[6]—The *Iliad* of Homer,[7] and—what do you call this? *Holding it up.*

Boston sharply: A bullet. It struck the book and saved my life.

French Pete: One bullet. No value? *Enter Skaggs, same business. Skaggs of Tuolumne, fifty dollars, a diamond pin, a pearl handled razor, and a bible. Enter Kentuck does not reappear at once—impatient movement from men.*

Boston: Oh! Come out of that. . . .

Skaggs: Wake him up. . . .

Miners: Smoke him out. *Kentuck appears at door, foolish and embarrassed, laughs nervously and examines his little finger held aloft. Motions to his comrades, who gather round him, shows them his finger.*

Kentuck: It rastled with my finger, the darned little cuss. He! He!

French Pete: Kentuck. *Kentuck starts, goes back to hat, examines his pockets vainly, turns them inside out, chuckles, stops, says "he rastled with my finger" and laughs. Remembers himself, runs to wings, brings his rifle and puts it in the hat, saying "he rastled with it." Attempts to reenter cabin, but is hustled good humouredly by the others. In the confusion Stumpy appears at the door.*

French Pete: Order, comrades!

Stumpy: It ain't my way to spoil sport, boys, and it ain't my way to disappoint this yer camp and go back on my word, and you know it, I leave it to you as far minded men if it ain't so. When I reckoned to open this yer sideshow this evening at the request of the chair, I kept suthing out of my calculations. That suthing, boys, was—Natur! From the indication and the way thing are pinting in there, there'll hev to be an intermission of ten minutes for refreshments. *Applause and cries of Aye Aye from Kentuck. Boston, Skaggs &c. who remain in groups by the cabin—the remainder who have not yet entered disperse with signs of disappointment. Stumpy who had reentered, appears at door with tin cup.*

Stumpy with finger to his lips: Lay low, and keep dark, boys, as little noise as possible until I get back. *Exit. Miner with notebook picks up hat and compares notes — then approaches Oakhurst and French Pete shaking the hat.*

Miner: Come down, gentlemen. Officers not exempt. *French Pete throws a fifty dollar slug carelessly.*

Oakhurst good humouredly: I'll see that fifty, Pete, and go twenty better — *throws it in the hat.*

French Pete: I'll see your twenty better and raise you thirty.

Oakhurst: Will you? Well, I'll see your thirty and raise you a hundred.

French Pete: Good. So this is your little game, Jack Oakhurst. *After searching vigorously in his pocket.* I see your hundred and — *excitedly* — go you five hundred and — hold on boys — that diamond pin, worth another five hundred better. *Writes on paper, hands it to Oakhurst.* There, that's a thousand all told — What you say? *Applause from miners who have gathered round.*

Oakhurst: I like your style, Pete. I'll see your five hundred dollars and your diamond pin — *producing diamond pin from shirt* — and I'll go you a diamond ring better — *taking one from his finger — To miner with hat.* There, rake down the pile. *Laughter and applause.*

French Pete: The devil on the luck.

Kentuck who has been lingering by door of cabin rushing excitedly to front: Silence, boys, silence.

French Pete: I only said — the devil take the luck. *Cry of child from cabin. French Pete starts back, miners fly to wings in ridiculous alarm.*

Kentuck frightened yet pleased: Don't be skeert, boys. It's only — only . . .

All: What?

Kentuck: It. . . . *pointing to cabin.*
French Pete angrily: It's a demoiselle. Can't you say *her*?
Dublin Bay: Ach! Would the likes of him know whether it's a father or a mother he is, anyway—
Skaggs: Suthing must be done.
Dublin Bay: Whist I have it. Three fingers of Old Bourbon and sugar—no lemon!
French Pete: Just leave alone the liquor. She wants to be amused. *Skaggs comes forward with a pack of cards.* No, you redhead of a woodpecker, do you think to get a bet out of that minor, under age. No, something to make a noise—shake something—shake your head and make your two ideas rattle. *Boston produces dice and dice box, laughing.* No, won't do, don't make enough jingle—why? Because naturally they are loaded.
Kentuck excitedly: Rattle some loose silver. *All feel their empty pockets—consternation. They approach cabin door cautiously and perform all manner of antics with a view to pacifying child.*
Oakhurst beckoning French Pete aside: Keep it up. Don't let the boys cool down. Don't let Boston talk them over. Don't let Skaggs get drunk for an hour if you can help it. *Listening.* What is that? *The sound of a fife and drum become more distinct—miners carrying a rude coffin are seen on the heights—to miners.* Steady, boys. *They turn round, see the funeral, all uncover their heads as Oakhurst and Pete have done and fall into attitudes of respect. Dublin Bay kneels and crosses himself, when funeral disappears they rise.* It's going on all right now. Before twenty minutes are over, we'll have that helpless infant a power here, and please God—a new life for Roaring Camp. *Exits direction of funeral. Miners about to resume antics, Stumpy comes from back with tin cup—disperses them at the door.*

Stumpy mysteriously: Now watch boys. Listen and observe the effects of maternal tenderness. *Enters cabin.*

Kentuck after listening effusively: Ah, boys! That's skill. Stumpy knows what's what. He's got his hand on the lever now.

French Pete: Yes, he's cut off the exhaust pipe. His fingers are not all thumbs, of that Stumpy. *Skaggs motions to Boston in dumb show that he wants a drink. They exit together unperceived.*

Kentuck musingly: I reckon it's all along of that wife of his in the States—the one he's always braggin' about.

Dublin Bay: Thrue for you. And its too pretty entirely she is for the likes of him.

Kentuck: Look at her photograph—he dropped one the other day—*exhibits it*—Just A-1. Looks like one o' them Frisco actresses.

French Pete aside: What she is I wager. Price fifty cents cabinet size colored. I never believed with two eyes shut in a Madame Stumpy. *Looking round.* But Skaggs and Boston are gone. I do not like that. It means whiskey for one and devilment for two.

Dungaree Jack entering hastily: There's a strange sail in the offing boys. She was sighted first in one of them settlements down on the river. They say it's a woman looking after her husband. Fellow shipmates, don't look skeert. *Men all slink away except French Pete and Kentuck.* Avast there! I don't suppose she's particular about which?

French Pete: How do you know this?

Dungaree Jack: Skaggs and Boston just spoken her.

French Pete aside: What can they want with her. I don't half like it. *Aloud.* Ah, here's Skaggs, *aside* and as much whiskey as he can carry.

Skaggs entering drunk: Ish all ri-te boys. She's comin'. The real thing. Goodbye, Stumpy. Goodbye, Jinny. Goodbye, Baby.

Kentuck seizing him: What do you mean, you drunken idiot?

Skaggs: All ri! I shay. Boston shays—all ri. All the boys shay—all ri. Boston asks woman to take baby and take hat. It's fair bargain. Baby goes to 'sylum or Water cure—no more of him in Roaring Camp. No more crying—no more peashful repose of Camp disturbed. No more John Oakhurst putting on airs and shpiling Camp. No more French Pete. No no . . . ta-ta ta-ta Baby. *Staggers off and exits Left.*

French Pete aside: So that is their little game. *To Kentuck aloud.* Listen, comrade. Is this child who first drew breath here to be given over to the first stranger that passes because it suits the selfishness of one man and the drunken idea of another. Eh?

Kentuck: Never! Never!

French Pete: Then do what I tell you. Stand behind that rock and watch, and let no one approach till I return. *Is about to go—pauses and sees Kentuck take out revolver and examine it.* He's good for a dozen men any day. But could he stand out against one of the fair sex. Humph! *Aloud calling back Kentuck.* Kentuck!

Kentuck: Well, Pete.

French Pete: You would not let any woman fool you? Eh? Twist you round eh? You know?

Kentuck: Not much.

French Pete: Not if she was beautiful? Young? A grand beauty like . . . like . . . Mrs. Stumpy?

Kentuck: You bet. . . . *seeing French Pete more anxiously.* But I say—I wouldn't use *that* to her, *pointing to pistol.* I wouldn't cuss her. What shall I do?

French Pete laughing: Why, amuse her. Play with her. Make love furiously, passionately. Fascinate her.

Kentuck: I see. *Dubiously.* But Pete, it is more in your line. Watch for her instead of me. You stay.

French Pete: Nonsense! Be a man. *Exits left. Kentuck reluctantly pockets revolver and retires behind the rock.*

Stumpy appears at cabin door: She sleeps at last. I thought she never would, thanks to that howling gang. Yet it's only the square thing to say that since that yer baby was born they've let up a heap in the yellin', and shoutin' that gave a name to Roaring Camp. I reckon there ain't been a free fight or a six shooter fired in three days. And they owe it all to me and my donkey Jinny. Ah! You little varmint, *apostrophising[8] baby through door,* don't forget what you owe to me and an ass—don't go back on your foster parents—*coming down stage.* I wonder what Mrs. Stumpy, supposing that noble woman ever allowed herself to be called by the name they give me here—would say, if she saw me now. Ha! Ha! Oh no! *I never could bring up a child. I couldn't rear a family. I couldn't be trusted even with one of my own twins, and now look at me, and that ass*—what a lesson to Mrs. Stumpy! I'd just like to see her here. *Stopping suddenly and meditating*—Would I? Well, not exactly *now.* I don't think she'd like to know that to keep up her reputation in the camp, to make my brag of her good with the boys, I've laid out five dollars on photographs of the prettiest actress I could find in Frisco. *Draws photo from his bosom.* And yet it's awfully flattering to Mary Frances—but women are ungrateful! Ah well. *Looking right—hides behind cabin.* Ah! You little varmint—*listening.* I suppose you'll be like the rest of them? *Enters cabin.*

Kentuck reappearing behind rock: I see no one—*perceives Stumpy—rushes up to him.* How is the d—d little cuss?

Stumpy importantly: Ah! The child! All right.

Kentuck: How did you do it?

Stumpy: It's easy enough when you know how—a little gentleness—kindness—a general sort o' lovingness like this—*imitates the dawdling of an infant.*

Kentuck: So! *Absurdly imitating him.*
Stumpy laughing: Why, you'd frighten the life out of her. Look at yer hands, man! Coarse, rough, dirty! Look at yer beard. Rough, dirty. Look at your shirt. Rough, coarse, dirty. Smell your clothes, man. Pipes and tobacco. Your breath. Pipes and whiskey.
Kentuck furiously, putting hand on pistol: Damnation. You dare. *Stumpy stops him with a gesture towards door.*
Kentuck frightened and apologetic: I was joking, Pard! But you *were* rough on me, weren't you? No. *Looking at himself.* It ain't clothes—there's John Oakhurst wears a biled shirt[9] every day, scents hisself, don't drink, cannot smoke—and yet he—well! *Loudly* I'm d—d—*stops.* I mean he did not dare to face her—*pointing to cabin.*
Stumpy: That's because he's not a family man. A man's got to have a woman about him to learn her ways and sorter copy from her. They fondle and caress you, till the first thing you know you've got the hang of it yourself.
Kentuck: I suppose you got those caressing ways from your wife?
Stumpy abstractedly: No. *Recovering himself.* Oh yes. She was a Siren,[10] you bet! She had a voice like a Bobolink, and nestled up agin you like a kitten. Ah! She was a beauty.
Kentuck: And why did you run away from her?
Stumpy excitedly: Who says I ran away?
Kentuck: Oh, I see! She ran away from you.
Stumpy furiously: You lop-eared fool.
Kentuck warningly: There, you razeed[11] light draught idiot. *Both men turn angrily to each other, begin to swear and wrangle but recollect themselves. Stumpy enters cabin.* The little beast might have died before that cantankerous crab would have moved.

Stumpy reappears at door with baby muffled up. Kentuck bends over it admiringly. Enter Mrs. Stumpy opposite wing facing Stumpy—sees and recognizes him.

Mrs. Stumpy *aside*: Gracious. My husband. William Henry Smith.

Stumpy *catching sight of her over Kentuck's bowed head*: My wife! The Devil! *Pushes back Kentuck and violently slams door of cabin in his face.*

Kentuck *amazed*: Halloo! What's up? Oh, I say, *knocking*—Open that door, Stumpy.

Mrs. Stumpy *watching aside*: Stumpy! Ah! An assumed name. Impostor.

Kentuck *still knocking*: Stumpy! Bring out your baby again!

Mrs. Stumpy *aside*: His Baby! Indeed! *Crossing to Kentuck—aloud.* Sir!

Kentuck *starting aside*: I see, the strange woman. I must keep her off. *Aloud* Yes, ma'am—y're looking for? *Prevents her from nearing cabin.*

Mrs. Stumpy *still trying to approach aside*: This brigand is evidently one of his creatures and suspects me. If I persist, he may become violent. *Aloud.* I was looking for . . .

Kentuck *interposing*: The fellow who lived here, ma'am,—oh, he's gone—yes, to the States—six months ago. *Aside.* Pete told me to be soft on her. *Aloud smirking.* It's a fine day, and— y're looking well!

Mrs. Stumpy *aside*: The creature is not so bad looking after all. I must try and soften him. He may reveal something. *Aloud.* Thank you. Can you tell me the name of the gentleman who *once* lived in that cabin?

Kentuck *aside*: What the devil shall I say? *Stepping between her and cabin.* If I tell her it's Stumpy, she may have heard Stumpy has the baby. *Aloud.* You see, it belongs to the camp, generally, but Dungaree Jack had it.

Mrs. Stumpy: Dungaree Jack! What a singular name!

Kentuck: Mebbee you're right, Miss. I reckon it does seem rather looney to a stranger. You see, Miss, most of the boys in Roaring Camp sorter left their names at home with their families, for safe keeping, I reckon, and took up the first nickname that they picked up, or was thrown at them. Now Dungaree Jack ain't got no call to that name except he was a sailor once, and wore Dungaree trousers. I beg your pardon, Miss. We've got French Pete, because he's Pierre suthing or other, and comes from France. That house yonder belongs to Dublin Bay.

Mrs. Stumpy: I see—built here, but owned in Ireland.

Kentuck: No, Miss! It's the name o' the song that chap is always singing. Now I'm from old Kentucky myself and they call me Kentuck.

Mrs. Stumpy: And your real name is?

Kentuck coolly: Of course, it ain't Kentuck.

Mrs. Stumpy: Really, and the gentleman I met just now whom they called Boston.

Kentuck: Only came from there. *Mrs. Stumpy impatiently tries to approach cabin, but is always intercepted by Kentuck who smirks and bows.*

Mrs. Stumpy: Then perhaps you never heard of Smith?

Kentuck approaching her: Smith! *Slapping her on the back with good natured familiarity.* Smith. Ah, now you're talking pardner. Why there was fourteen Smiths killed here last year, in one free fight, and I reckon, the fact is, this year the name ain't so popular. But you mustn't go away with the idea that all the men in Roaring Camp are named after their places. Why, there's Stumpy. *Aside* Oh! Well, I've put my foot in it.

Mrs. Stumpy aside: He looks disturbed. *Aloud*—Stumpy! Well, Sir?

Kentuck: Well! You see, Stumpy—he—he, well, Stumpy is Stumpy.

Mrs. Stumpy: Go on.

Kentuck: Yes. You see he's stiff in one leg—and it's shorter than the other.

Mrs. Stumpy aside: William Henry under an assumed name—the villain. There cannot be another wife afflicted with an unequal legged husband. *Aloud eagerly.* Go on please.

Kentuck aside piteously: But I can't. *Aloud.* Ah, he's gone! Gone to the States.

Mrs. Stumpy ironically: Ah! Ah! Like Dungaree Jack.

Kentuck coolly: Gone home to his wife.

Mrs. Stumpy: To his wife!

Kentuck: I said so. And an almighty slick, peart,[12] handsome woman, you bet.

Mrs. Stumpy pleased: Then you have seen her?

Kentuck: Well, the photograph that he totes round, and gives the boys. *Exhibits photograph.*

Mrs. Stumpy: What's this? *Aside.* Another female! *Aloud.* So he says this is his wife, does he?

Kentuck: I reckon.

Mrs. Stumpy aside: The old bigamist. I'll expose him. Ugh! *Claws the air wrathfully in direction of cabin.*

Kentuck insinuatingly: Purty, eh?

Mrs. Stumpy shortly: Hideous!

Kentuck: Well, now do you know I reckon she looks suthing like you. Not such a fine figure—but just them eyes. Giddier, of course, and more colty. Wants yer dignity. Ma'am! But like you. *Aside.* That's fetching her. *Enter Boston, Skaggs drunk, and other miners.*

Boston to Mrs. Stumpy: I see you have lost no time in finding the place with the assistance doubtless of this gentleman. Let us be prompt. We have no time to lose. These gentlemen who accompany me are our principal citizens.

Skaggs drunkenly: Our very first shitizens.

Boston: They endorse freely the proposition I made you an hour ago, and are ready to deliver the child in your hands. They expect you to take it to San Francisco and bring it up at their expense, for which purpose they advance you now the proceeds of a public subscription amounting to over two thousand dollars. *Motion to miner who brings in hat.*

Kentuck violently: It's a lie. Stand back there Boston or—*draws revolver.*

Boston: Before a lady.

All: Before a lady. *Seize and disarm him.*

Boston: Pardon me, but you must see the necessity of hurrying away the child from scenes of violence like these. Lose no time—a horse is ready, saddled at the foot of the hill. I myself will accompany you beyond the confines of this camp.

Mrs. Stumpy aside: Perhaps I can learn more. *Aloud.* But, Sir, you forget I have a sacred mission to fulfill. I must find my lost husband.

Kentuck hastily to miners: That's so, boys. She's seeking her husband, do you hear? Is there any mean skunk among ye, would try to make her go back on her word?

Miners hesitating: There's suthing in that.

Boston: Far be it from me, from any of us, Madam, to turn you from your sacred trust. But since I saw you, I have exhausted all enquiry. Your husband is no longer here.

Mrs. Stumpy aside: He lies—it is a shameful conspiracy.

Boston continuing: He has returned to the States to seek you. Let that child take his place in your distant home, a new bond of union which you shall rear as your own.

Mrs. Stumpy aside: As my own! Never! I do not like this haste. *Aloud* Really Sir, I . . .

Kentuck eagerly: Don't believe him, Miss! Don't take stock in him—he's lying!

Mrs. Stumpy: Why you told me yourself my husband was gone. *Aside,* I must see by myself—*Aloud to Boston.* Before I consent I must see the child.

Boston: Enter here, Madam, and behold the helpless orphan. *Mrs. Stumpy enters looking triumphantly at Kentuck who stands by the door abashed. Boston and others walk off opposite direction lighting cigars etc. As his wife disappears Stumpy is seen emerging from chimney on roof in great distress unperceived by others.*

Stumpy: Thank God, I have dodged her. If Kentuck could help me away. *To Kentuck.* Pst! Psh! *Kentuck looks up. Dumb show. Mrs. Stumpy rushes out exclaiming "He was not there"—catches sight of Kentuck gesticulating, looks up, sees Stumpy, shakes her fist at him, is about to call out, changes her mind and walks resolutely up to Boston.*

Mrs. Stumpy with side look at roof: Sir, I have decided. I accept. *Movement of Boston to hurry her—stops him.* On one condition—I will not deprive the child of the care of her last surviving parent.

Boston: Her parent?

Mrs. Stumpy: Her father.

Boston: Let me explain, Ma'am. You have mistaken the nurse for the father. Disabuse your mind of the thought that that gentleman is its father—*oratorically*—only as we all are the fathers of the orphan. Are we not, boys?

Miners: We are that.

Mrs. Stumpy aside: Can I believe him, yet William Henry always was such a fool. *Aloud* But . . .

Boston interrupting: Stumpy took care of the child from the first, when the wretched mother died in his arms.

Mrs. Stumpy: In his arms?

Stumpy on roof: Put his foot in it again.

Mrs. Stumpy aside: I shall find out more. *Aloud.* No matter. I remain here.

Stumpy: I knew she would.

Boston: And your husband, whom you have not found, whom you must seek elsewhere! Your unhappy husband.

Stumpy feelingly: Unhappy! Oh yes.

Mrs. Stumpy glancing at Stumpy: My husband! From this moment I consecrate myself to this child, and . . . I renounce my husband forever.

Boston: The devil! *Turns to Skaggs and others and consults with them.*

Stumpy: Halloo! I wonder if she means it. I'll try her. *Slides down and reappears on stage from back of cabin. Approaching Mrs. Stumpy slyly — she starts — he whispers warningly.* Keep it up. At your peril. Confess to our relations and you're a dead woman.

Mrs. Stumpy frightened: He means it — He looks desperate — Leave me.

Boston: It is impossible for you to remain here, Madam, your offer is madness. *Approval of Stumpy.* Think of your reputation. What would your husband say?

Stumpy hypocritically: What would your husband say? *Aside.* Cut and run. *Miners have been coming in dressed as for a gala day.*

Oakhurst entering in evening dress: He would know that an honest woman would be protected from insult in Roaring Camp. Is it not so, gentleman?

All: Aye! Aye!

Boston surveying miners sarcastically: What is the meaning of this masquerade? Is it to honour a possible successor to Cherokee Sal? *Kentuck and others rush to strike Boston.*

All: Shame.

Oakhurst interposing: Stop—Are you mad?

Skaggs reluctantly releasing Boston: Didn't you say that an honest woman was safe from insult in this yer camp?

Kentuck: And wasn't it allowed that no one was to go back on Cherokee Sal—our baby's mother?

Oakhurst to Boston: A majority of the men of Roaring Camp having resolved to adopt a child as their own, are here to see it decently done, and stand as sponsors to the child at its Christening. Am I right, gentlemen?

All: Right.

Kentuck to French Pete looking at his clothes: Will these yer duds do?

French Pete dubiously: Well, you do not look elegant enough to take a first pew. *Exit with Kentuck.*

Oakhurst: As it is the intention of this camp *not* to part with the child on any consideration, there is no reason why the kind offer of this lady should not be gratefully received, and that she be declared now and forever an honourable member of this camp with all its privileges. What say you gentlemen?

All: Aye.

Stumpy in alarm: But.

Mrs. Stumpy pinching him aside: Not a word! *Moves from him.*

Oakhurst: Be quiet, you fool. You won't be parted from the baby. I'll recommend you to the lady, though she don't seem to take kindly to you. *Follows Mrs. Stumpy and converses with her.*

Boston to Stumpy: Don't show your jealousy so plainly, man. Give the poor woman a show. Ha! Ha! We won't tell Mrs. Stumpy. *Exits laughing.*

Stumpy lugubriously aside: I might bolt with the baby. But she'd tell all, and they'd pursue me. If I could only see her for a moment alone and explain—and pacify her. It's no use trying to catch her eye. It's such an eye! When I do, I catch it.

Oakhurst to Mrs. Stumpy: Until a suitable cabin can be built for you, you will temporarily occupy . . .
All: Take mine! Take mine.
Oakhurst: You will temporarily occupy Mr. Stumpy's, who will at once vacate it. As he had the care of the child, if he can assist you in any way.
Stumpy eagerly: Certainly, surely. I'll come in with you. *Going towards cabin.* I'll show you all the things.
Mrs. Stumpy freezingly: Sir!
Stumpy low pleadingly: But Mary Frances . . .
Mrs. Stumpy moving him away: Retire! *Low* Do not Mary Frances me! *Enters slowly, gazing fiercely at Stumpy, holds the door a moment. Stumpy offers to enter—slams it in his face.*
Dublin Bay admiringly: Now that's what I call an honest woman.
Dungaree Jack: Stumpy, I'm ashamed of you.
Kentuck: Such freedom to a stranger.
French Pete: What would your wife say, eh?
Stumpy: What will she say? *Exits.*
Oakhurst: Order, gentlemen. *Miners again come to order as before.*
Oakhurst beside barrel: When this meeting adjourned an hour ago, there were some little differences in regard to the disposition of this child, a few gentlemen preferring that it should be brought up outside this camp against the wishes of the majority. These differences were adjusted, ten minutes since in the wood yonder, one at four hundred yards, the other at twenty paces. A fair distance, gentlemen, I believe.
All: That's square. A good distance.
Oakhurst: Luck, which has been with us since the birth of that child, sent us at the same moment the one being necessary to its helplessness. She has offered to live with us, and devote herself to the child. Shall we, gentlemen, accept the double trust?

All: Aye! Aye!

Boston entering in evening dress: Yes. Yes! *Markedly.*

Oakhurst: Then it is our duty to make suitable provision for our adopted child now and hereafter. What say you gentlemen, to each man giving one fifth of his yearly income?

Skaggs who entered after Boston: Make it half, boys.

Dublin Bay: He speaks for himself—it's the half of nothing he's after giving.

Oakhurst: One fifth, gentlemen, is sufficient, if you pledge your word for it.

Boston: Poor child! It cannot live on barren pledges.

Oakhurst: Do you pledge? Gentlemen?

All: We pledge.

Oakhurst: In luck or out of luck, in prosperity or misfortune you pledge.

All: In luck or out of luck, in prosperity or misfortune we pledge. *Pause. Cries outside of Gold! Gold! Hurrah! Commotion in meeting.*

Oakhurst: Order! Clear away these men.

Enter miner panting, and shaking hands with men: Gold, boys! Hurrah! We've struck it rich.

All: Where?

Miners: In the grave of Cherokee Sal.

Dublin Bay: Ach! Go away with ye!

French Pete entering after miner: It is the truth. When the grave was filled, the last lump of earth thrown, broke and showed the sparks of the gold. *Waving his hand.* It is not all. Not only the grave where the poor woman sleeps but the whole mountain is veined and yellow with gold. *All rise and seize shovels and picks.*

Oakhurst: Stand back, boys! And hear me. If this is true, from her grave the mother has shown us the legacy of the child. Until we can rear to that nameless woman a monument dedicated to the benefactress of Roaring Camp, it must remain sacred. Sit down. The gold will not run away from us with Cherokee Sal to watch it. *All sit.* Now, gentlemen, shall we renew our pledges?

All: We will.

Oakhurst: Then let us christen the child as becomes the heiress of Roaring Camp. *Door of cabin opens and discovers Mrs. Stumpy stiff and rigid, overdressed in loud finery carrying baby. Stumpy appears meekly, dressed in old fashioned blue coat with gilt buttons. Miners bring in, like a litter, a sluice box, decorated with boughs and flowers.*

Dungaree Jack nudging Stumpy: You've got 'em all on Stumpy.

French Pete: You are dazzling.

Stumpy sternly: Order at the christening. *Aside.* My wedding suit. I thought it might fetch her—but it doesn't. *Child is placed in box in center. Mrs. Stumpy beside it. Stumpy behind. Miners grouped round it. Oakhurst and French Pete at the head. Skaggs whispers to his neighbour, who whispers to Kentuck. Pause. Miners grow impatient. Cries of "Go on," "It's your play," &c.*

Oakhurst: An important feature has been forgotten—the name. Have you any to suggest?

Skaggs: George Washington.

French Pete: Antoinette.[13] *Different cries of Eclipse, Lady Jane, Blanche Augusta.*

Stumpy very loud looking at Mrs. Stumpy who turns her head away: Mary Jane. *Aside.* No! It won't wash. *"Flying Scud," "Columbia" mixed with cries of No, No from various miners.*

French Pete: Silence. Give her a name that belongs to her. She brought the luck to Roaring Camp. Call her "Luck." It is very simple.

Oakhurst: Remember she must have a name she can grow up upon—perhaps marry upon. *Cries of "never," "no marrying," "shan't give consent."*

Boston: French Pete's idea is a good one—gentlemen, accept it with a modification. You cannot call a young lady "the Luck of Roaring Camp," but we can borrow the language of the soil, and call her in good Spanish "La Fortuna del Campo Clamoroso." *Cries of "That's your sort," "Bully pour vous," "Three cheers for Fortuna."*

Skaggs drunkenly: Forty niner! that's good. The forty niner of Roaring Camp.

Dublin Bay: Forty for short.

Stumpy with gravity: I do proclaim you La Fortuna del Campo Clamoroso, Forty for short, according to the laws of the United States, and the State of California. So help me God!

Tableau
Curtain
End of Prologue.

Characters in Acts I and II.

Colonel John Oakhurst   U.S. Legation in Paris, formerly *Jack Oakhurst*

Joseph Adams   American Banker in Paris, formerly *Boston*

William Henry Smith   Proprietor of the Universal Hotel San Francisco, formerly *Stumpy*

Jim Skaggs   Capitalist and teetotaller

Dick Scott   Practical miner and expert of the Sierra mine, formerly *Kentuck*

Baron de Trempes   Secret financial agent of the Sierra mine in France, almost ruined

Paul de Lussan   A young French officer in the *Chasseurs d'Afrique*, in love with Fortuna

Fortuna del Campo Clamoroso   The Luck of Roaring Camp

Marquise de Lussan   Mother of Paul de Lussan

Madame Pomercy   Rich young widow, friend of Mr. Adams, niece of Marquise de Lussan

Mrs. Stompee Smith   A fashionable member of the American colony in Paris, formerly *Mrs. Smith*

Madame Joubard   An ambitious French parvenue.[14]

Antoinette Joubard   Her daughter.

Zélie   Maid to *Mme Pomercy*.

Marie   Maid to *Mrs. Smith*

Act I

The villa Pomercy at St. Germain[15] near Paris.

A lapse of seventeen years between Prologue and Act I.

Villa Pomercy at St. Germain near Paris. A large room opening at flat by two windows on a balcony and a French window with steps to garden beyond. Left entrance to conservatory. Right folding doors. The room is tastefully furnished in the Parisian style, curtains and portières[16] of gay actonne, curtained recess, fire place, couches, tables, jardinières.[17] At one table Left Marquise de Lussan sitting, doing some knitting. At another table Right, Madame Joubard poring over a book. Madame Pomercy seated between them with another volume.

Madame Joubard, *after a silence closing her book:* I was sure of it! *Triumphantly.* I knew it. In the whole noblesse of Spain, there is not a family of Del Campo Clamoroso.
Madame Pomercy, *shutting her book:* I see nothing about them here. Still, I repeat that my banker, Adams, assured me that Mademoiselle Fortuna is of Spanish descent.
Madame Joubard: Ta, ta, ta. Mr. Adams is an American, and what do those republicans know of descent, of titles of Blood! Blue Blood! Why, they have not a drop themselves.
Marquise *looking up:* Not one drop? How melancholy. And yet an interesting natural phenomenon. While you, dear Madame Joubard . . .
Madame Joubard *interrupting effusively:* Yes, Marquise. I adore the aristocracy. I worship it. I have lived in it as a girl, and wife, and widow.

Marquise: You are too kind, dear Madame, such disinterestedness. *Aside.* Her father was a shop keeper, her husband a wholesale dealer in cheap champagnes, her brother . . . *Aloud.* Apropos dear Madame, what news of your brother-in-law? Do you ever hear from him?

Madame Joubard: You mean Pierre?—The one who ran away to America years ago—no! Thank God—never!

Marquise: Ah, pardon—*aside*—the best of the lot, for he ran away from the rest.

Madame Pomercy: So really, no mention, of . . .

Madame Joubard: Not a word. Plenty of Campos, which means field, country, camp. I looked it up in the Dictionary. Fields of all descriptions. Campos early—late—joyful, of Iron &c, but not a single Campo Clamoroso.

Madame Pomercy: It did strike me, I own, as most uncommon.

Madame Joubard: Say impossible. From beginning to end. Fortuna! A heathenish Christian name. Fortuna. Of the Screeching Field. No decent blood can circulate under so outrageous a combination.

Marquise: It is not every one, dear Madam, who has the gift of calling their children by so euphonious a name as you gave your daughter.

Madame Joubard flattered: Antoinette! Yes, it is distinguished, legitimate, royal.

Marquise: Antoinette Joubard—A poem!

Madame Pomercy deprecatingly: Dear Aunt!

Madame Joubard: Fancy calling a girl "Money." Well, that in Fortuna's case it is not a misnomer. She is a Croesus,[18] I understand. For all that I should not have put Antoinette to the Sacré Coeur[19] had I known that pupils were admitted with so little enquiry. *To Madame Pomercy.* In our time the Sisters exercised more discrimination, dear Adèle.

Madame Pomercy wincing: Hardly! I think, *pointedly*, dear Madame Joubard.

Madame Joubard: As an old convent friend of yours, let me use the privilege of friendship to tell truths which others keep from you.

Marquise aside: Unsparingly she will use it, too. *Aloud*. Well.

Madame Joubard: You are more than imprudent in admitting to your intimacy, a girl of whom, in point of fact, you know nothing.

Madame Pomercy: Except that she is Adams' ward—and *significantly* the bosom friend and chosen companion of your daughter at the Sacré Coeur. See how pleased they were to meet again here.

Madame Joubard: I was not—I disliked the friendship. This foreign girl imports foreign notions, foreign ways. She will inoculate Antoinette with her subversive views.

Marquise laughing: You are a pessimist, dear Madame. What has the child done? What is she doing?

Madame Joubard: Say, rather, what does she leave undone? She rides without a groom, swims, talks loud, laughs till the tears run down her cheeks, and . . . and . . . she is disgracefully enthusiastic.

Marquise: Is that all? She is young and happy, she is neither ashamed of her youth, or afraid to show her happiness. She is natural. It is rare, but not wrong.

Madame Pomercy: Not wrong perhaps, dearest Aunt, but not sanctioned by our world—and you should not encourage her, by your partiality.

Marquise: But I will, my niece. I consider it my duty not to let you spoil her, and make her after your image. Between you all, you have created a code of manners which kills originality. We die of anemia in the starched platitude of our lives.

Puppets ourselves we breed puppets. Give *me* flesh & blood.

Madame Joubard viciously: Flesh and blood that flirt, that makes eyes at men—at your son Paul—at . . .

Marquise aside: Where is the crime? *Aloud—quietly.* Fortuna flirts, you say.

Madame Joubard: Outrageously. Would you like an American and a heretic as a daughter-in-law, Marquise?

Madame Pomercy: You look too far ahead.

Marquise coldly: My son is not thinking of marriage as yet. *Gaily—* he shows good taste in admiring a pretty girl, be it Fortuna or Antoinette.

Madame Joubard: Antoinette! God forbid. My daughter will accept the husband I select, but *she* does not flirt. She is shy, timid, modest.

Madame Pomercy politely: Mademoiselle Joubard will be a model wife, as she is a pattern daughter.

Marquise aside: Barring the wild oats, late crops are more plentiful. *Aloud.* Without detracting from Antoinette's merits I confess that I like the other girl with her fearless eyes, her rippling laughter, and frank brusquerie—she gladdens my old eyes and quickens the pulses of this tedi . . . very sedate interior.

Madame Joubard: Has Mademoiselle *ironically*—Mademoiselle Fortuna del Campo Clamoroso, no Mother, no Father, no relatives here or elsewhere?

Madame Pomercy: She is, I believe, an orphan, the ward of Mr. Adams, and after a fashion of Mrs. Smith—the Mrs. Stompee Smith, who burst upon the American colony with such splendour. We all know her—went there—and . . . dropped her—as one drops the foreign salons when they become a trifle too mixed. For that same reason, Adams, who is propriety itself, wished to remove Fortuna, who is grown up now, from that doubtful chaperone. I owe a debt of gratitude to the banker, he is out of pure and old friendship endeavouring to find out for me particulars of the Sierra mine. You remember that, against his advice and at de Trempes' suggestion I took shares in this concern which is either a fraud or a swindle. It was only a slight return to ask Fortuna here, when she seemed to wish it.

Marquise: She has proved quite an acquisition.

Madame Joubard: May you always think so. I only advise you to keep your eyes open as I have mine—for she shall not, I assure you, inoculate Antoinette with American customs. *Aside.* Nor catch the Baron de Trempes.

Madame Pomercy, piqued at last: Dear Madame Joubard, if anyone in this house is objectionable to you, pray let me release you from the promise you made to honour me with your company for a week.

Marquise with mock politeness: We should never forgive ourselves if Mademoiselle Antoinette . . .

Madame Joubard, hastily interrupting: Dear Adèle, I was jesting. Marquise, you misunderstand—my anxiety is all for the poor girl herself—the world—society. . . . *Aside* Go! And lose my chance of bringing the Baron to propose . . . not for all the Screeching Fields in the world.

Marquise: Let us drop the subject. Nay, more—a fine of two francs to be levied on whoever speaks except with kindness of my niece's unprotected guest. Ladies, do you agree? *She rises, puts away her knitting.* Well, it's a compact. . . . *Aside.* Your envy and ill nature must swell my poor box. . . . *Aloud.* Have you seen the illustrated papers? *They all move to furthest table and turn over books and photos while Baron de Trempes enters from garden with Antoinette dressed in the elegant but very simple style of a French girl with a garden hat trimmed with a wreath of flowers and flowers in her hand. They converse at the French window unseen as they think by the three ladies. Madame Joubard notices them, and prevents the other two from observing them—she is triumphant.*

Baron gallantly: Mademoiselle, I am in luck indeed when a fairy crowned with flowers meets me at the gates after a long and dusty drive.

Antoinette coyly: I was walking down the avenue . . . oh, quite accidentally . . . when your dog cart stopped.

Baron: Accidentally? Only?

Antoinette coquettishly: I overheard some one . . . oh, quite by chance—say you might come today.

Baron aside: She fibs—*Aloud.* How good of you to remember—*touching the flowers.* Can you spare me this rose . . . by chance?

Antoinette the same: Do you really care for it? *Hands it to him.*

Baron: Oh! Not like that. *Antoinette is about to place the flower in his button hole when the Marquise, who has quietly been watching the pair and been looking from them to Madame Joubard, bursts out laughing. Antoinette drops the rose, makes a demure curtsy and stands motionless.*

Marquise: From any other than your daughter I should call this a pretty lot of flirting. *Aside.* Bless the child, she is not all sawdust after all.

Madame Joubard with affected severity: Antoinette come here. *Low to her.* What made you come in now? *They talk low.*

Baron slightly shrugging his shoulders advances with exaggerated politeness to Madame Pomercy: Madame, I feel I am importunate, and you have a perfect right to drive me away, but my excuse lies in the attractions of the Villa Pomercy.

Madame Pomercy: Pray do not apologize. We should feel flattered that you do not find the distance between Paris and St. Germain an insuperable obstacle to visiting.

Marquise: Flattering indeed, that at the height of the racing season, you forsake for us your favourite haunts.
Baron: Looking around you, Marquise, can you wonder?
Antoinette aside: He looked at me.
Madame Joubard aside: He did not look at Antoinette.
Marquise: He means Fortuna.
Madame Pomercy: Apropos, Baron, have you heard the rumour about the Sierra Mine—your mine?
Baron starting: No! No! *Recovering himself.* Do not believe all you hear. *Following Madame Pomercy to opposite side where they sit down and talk. Aside.* She cannot know or suspect me?
Marquise to Antoinette: Dear child, what have you done with your friend?
Antoinette: I left her in the flower garden . . . alone—with Monsieur Paul.
Marquise: When you went to meet the Baron alone?
Antoinette: Oh, they do not mind it at all—they like it.
Madame Joubard: No doubt *she* does. And was she making eyes at him?
Marquise: Oh, I give you warning. Beware of the fine!
Antoinette: No! They were quarrelling.
Madame Pomercy looking up: Who was quarrelling?
Marquise: Never mind—only sparring!
Madame Pomercy: Oh, that leads to nothing—*Resumes talk with Baron.*
Marquise aside: Every road leads to Rome—*Aloud.* Come, I see, dear Mme Joubard, you are burning to act as peace-maker between the belligerents—your vocation! Am I right?
Madame Joubard: It is time some one should interfere and bring the . . . the . . . disgraceful . . . *Marquise puts out her hand as if for fine.*

Madame Joubard: I mean, watch over the American. *Moves with Marquise to centre door, to Antoinette audibly, seeing the Baron look up.* I trust, my daughter, you will never commit the indiscretion of meeting a man . . . alone!

Antoinette regretfully: Oh Mama, how could I—*Aside.* If I only dared, like Forty.

Madame Joubard: Follow us, Antoinette—a young girl's place is under her mother's wing—till she leaves it for a husband's protection. *Exit with Antoinette looking longingly at the Baron's tête-à-tête[20] with Madame Pomercy.*

Baron laughing: Bravo, Madame Joubard! A noble sentiment.

Madame Pomercy half ironically: Do you applaud a future mother-in-law? I have fancied you had views in that quarter.

Baron aside: Before the little heiress put into the shade the dot[21] of Mademoiselle Antoinette—*Aloud* God forbid! I have other ideas in my mind, other feelings in my heart.

Madame Pomercy: Your? You said your . . .

Baron: My heart.

Madame Pomercy: Did you? I thought you must have made a mistake. Well?

Baron: I am in love.

Madame Pomercy: You? How rich is she?

Baron: Do not be satirical. I could not see Mademoiselle del Campo and not be captivated by her charms, her beauty, her intellect.

Madame Pomercy: Yes, she is . . . immensely wealthy.

Baron eagerly: You are certain of it. *Recovering himself.* Not that I care. When two hearts are drawn together . . .

Madame Pomercy interrupting: Money is a powerful cement. . . . But, Baron, are you serious *this* time?

Baron: Never more so.

Madame Pomercy: The world does not always calumniate—and it credits you with some adventures, many flirtations, one or two virtuous efforts to settle down and reform—and several failures.

Baron: Is it generous to remind me of those, Madam? . . . I have resolved to offer Mademoiselle Fortuna my heart, my hand, and my title.

Madame Pomercy: Let us sum up—a heart slightly damaged, neatly repaired—a hand, . . . what shall we say of the hand?

Baron: That it can serve a friend, and strike a foe.

Madame Pomercy aside: From behind. *Aloud.* A title nobly borne . . . by your ancestors—illustrated by you on the race course, at the Stock Exchange, in various speculations. The present generation calls it regilding one's escutcheon.[22] Has the gilt worn off, that you try another process . . . matrimony?

Baron aside: She does not know how true she speaks. *Aloud.* Laugh at me if you will, but help me. Mademoiselle del Campo has neither Father nor Mother—she is under your care—plead my cause. Soon . . . at once.

Madame Pomercy laughing: Why, this is the ardour of a boy of twenty—not the deliberate wooing of a man of the world. Besides Mademoiselle Fortuna has Guardians.

Baron: I know! Adams the banker, who favours me, rather. *Aside.* But who will not when this accursed mine bubble bursts— *Aloud.* Mrs. Smith, where I first saw the girl during the holidays . . . but I depend on you. You do not, cannot know how much I have staked on that card.

Madame Pomercy: Gambler! There talks the habitué[23] of Hamburg, Baden, Monte Carlo.

Baron gallantly: Monte Carlo, of which I keep the most charming memories. I met you there.

Madame Pomercy: And broke the bank.

Baron: Lucky at cards—unlucky in love—you had so disdainfully crushed. . . .

Madame Pomercy: Your weak attempt at love making—an allegiance divided with *contemptuously*—the green cloth. No, Baron, as an acquaintance.

Baron: Say friend.

Madame Pomercy: No, I keep to my word—as an acquaintance, a gambler is passable and possible—as a suitor, not.

Baron piqued: You forget in this sweeping condemnation of my pursuits that I saw you, Madame, at that same Monte Carlo, openly, uncompromisingly adjure your creed, and own to an enthusiastic admiration for the most notorious gambler who ever sat at roulette table in the two hemispheres.

Madame Pomercy, losing her negligent caustic tone: You mean the American? Well, yes? I admired the man who simply, nobly made himself the advocate of the widow and orphans. *Your* luck and your success that night had been ruin and death to the poor foolish wretch who had staked the last piece of bread of his family and lost it. He blew his brains out as he left the table where you counted your gain, a beggared, perhaps a dishonoured man.

Baron: Was I responsible for a mad man's suicide?

Madame Pomercy: Was the American? Less than you, I presume, but when the news of the tragedy spread, he took up a hat, poured into it his own winnings, and ever so much besides, and quietly offering to all the bystanders, compelled them by the magnetism of example to swell the sum he was collecting for the stricken mourners.

Baron: And the Casino rang with the rumour that the proud Madame Pomercy unclasped from her wrist a valuable bracelet, and threw it with her purse into the hat—rumour added that the jewel so promptly given was not handed over to the recipients of the fascinating foreigner's largesse.

Madame Pomercy: Because I found my bracelet the next morning on my dressing table with an unsigned note "An ornament bearing in full your name 'Adèle' must not be offered for sale by strangers. Rest assured that our protégés are none the poorer for this restitution." I shall never forgive myself for not finding out the name of a man so refined & so chivalrous.

Baron: Your Don Quixote left Monte Carlo the next day — But Madame, you have not yet promised me your assistance.

Madame Pomercy aside: Fortuna might do worse. He *cannot* be too particular about antecedents. *Aloud.* Stay to dinner, pay your court — and if a word from me to Adams . . .

Baron kissing her hand: A word from you has magic power.

Madame Pomercy: Well, you will find your idol — your *golden* idol in the grounds. . . . I do not detain you, impetuous lover. I myself have a letter to write.

Baron moving towards the garden — aside: My foot is in the stirrup. But I have no time to lose. *Exit.*

Madame Pomercy looking after him, and entering doors on Right: Why did he bring up that incident of Monte Carlo . . . which I so vainly try to forget. . . . *Exits.*

Enter from conservatory, Servant preceding Boston & Oakhurst: This way gentlemen. *to Boston.* I shall inform Madame that Monsieur Adams is here.

Boston: And give her this card. . . . Colonel Oakhurst. *Exit servant.*

Oakhurst: You are treated as an habitué, entirely, old fellow, and if the widow is as *comme il faut*[24] as her surroundings you are as lucky now at St. Germain, as you used to be at Roaring Camp. I say, old man, what do you suppose she'd say to the little red wood shanty, and the two pork barrels — the counter where the great American Banker, Adams, then known as Boston, cashed his first draft and made his first loan?

Boston: I'm afraid she'd say that first loan was a risky beginning.

Oakhurst: Ah! Why so?

Boston: Because if I remember rightly, it was to the Honourable Colonel John Oakhurst, first Secretary of Legation of the United States of America, then plain Jack Oakhurst, the reckless gambler, and—without security.

Oakhurst laughing: By Jove! You're right—and that act I remember, too, wiped out our old grudges and differences about the Luck! Apropos, while I have kept the run of nearly all of her old guardians. Skaggs and Stumpy are, we know, still in San Francisco. I have heard nothing lately of Kentuck. Has his continuous ill luck culminated in something serious?

Boston: I hope not. But I confess, I should not at this present time deeply regret any slight misfortune that kept him and some of his brother guardians from Paris. To be frank with you I dislike their possible influence on Fortuna. Already I have deemed it best to remove her for a while from the roof of Mrs. Smith, where the associations were hardly suited to the position she should occupy.

Oakhurst sarcastically: Humph! I see! Stumpy, Skaggs, Kentuck, and Mrs. Stumpy don't quite step with a Lussan, Pomercy, Joubard, &c. &c. But come, we cannot in the interest of Fortuna entirely put the past aside, especially not Kentuck.

Boston: And why?

Oakhurst: You shall hear. At Fredericksburg, the Confederate Regiment that most gallantly contested our right was led by a Colonel Pierre. Mortally wounded, he was taken prisoner but would deliver his sword to no one but me. When I rode up to the ambulance I recognized in the dying man, whom I had been fighting all day—French Pete.

Boston: The fortune of war. He sympathized with the South. But what does that matter?

Oakhurst: Not much to you who were laying the basis of your wealth as Commissary general in the same corps with myself; much to me who had to receive the last words of the old friend I had helped to slay. "Seek out Kentuck," he gasped, "he has my last message to the Luck. God bless her," & died in my arms.

Boston: And to get this message delivered, which can only revive dark days of Fortuna's youth, you are seeking Kentuck. I have done better. I have used my influence with Madame Pomercy to induce her to act as chaperone to Fortuna and introduce her to *her* world.

Oakhurst: In other words, to supplant her old friend Mrs. Stumpy—whose faults we all know—and replace her by a Parisian widow, whose artificially polished interior is a glass in which you see your folly, but not hers. I prefer Mrs. Smith.

Boston: But she has become loud, fast, flaunting her would-be flirtations . . .

Oakhurst: While your widow, no doubt, conceals some unorthodox passion. So you have asked me here to endorse this transfer of Fortuna?

Boston: Not quite that. I want your experience in a more practical matter. *Briefly.* At the recommendation of some fool or knave Madame Pomercy has invested in the Sierra Mine. What do you know of it?

Oakhurst: A worn out fraud, galvanised into life by some American experts, and rouged and powdered by some European "Chevalier d'Industrie."[25]

Boston: I feared as much. But can it be returned?

Oakhurst: Not unless the chief agent in Europe can be identified. He is said to be a man of position, titled I believe, who will refund to avoid exposure and disgrace. I am on his track. This is part of my business in Paris.

Boston: Then you are exactly the man most welcome to the pretty widow at this juncture. Devote yourself to her service and win eternal gratitude.

Oakhurst: I never met but one woman for whose gratitude I would have cared. Ah. *Sighs. He draws back a little as doors Right open and Madame Pomercy enters. Boston steps forward to meet her.*

Boston: Dear Madame Pomercy.

Oakhurst: Good Heavens. The woman of the bracelet.

Madame Pomercy stepping forward: Forgive me, Adams, for keeping you waiting, and excuse me to your friend. *Aside seeing Oakhurst.* The American of Monte Carlo.

Boston introducing: My friend, Colonel Oakhurst of the American Legation and Fortuna's guardian. *Oakhurst bows low.*

Madame Pomercy coming to him with outstretched hand: Providence of orphans and widows, restorer of lost goods. Welcome to the villa of Pomercy, Colonel, and thank you for giving me an opportunity of paying a longstanding debt.

Oakhurst kissing her hand: Madame, absolve me of any premeditation.

Madame Pomercy aside regretfully: Only an accident! *Aloud to Boston.* This is a charming surprise.

Boston: I am thoroughly mystified. You know each other. *To Oakhurst.* Why this mystery?

Madame Pomercy: I shall explain. *They retire to Left and talk. Enter Baron with Antoinette laughing.*

Baron: There will be a row. *Aside seeing Oakhurst.* Don Quixote on friendly terms with Adams. I do not like this. *Enter Marquise trying to pacify Madame Joubard, who is in a violent state of exasperation.*

Marquise: After all. We can survive it.

Madame Joubard: It is incredible. Scandalous. Outrageous.

Antoinette: Really, Mamma, there is no harm.

Madame Joubard: Do not defend her, my angel! *Aside.* Before the Baron, too.

Madame Pomercy: What is it about? Are you hurt? Why this excitement?

Madame Joubard: I trust you will exercise your authority as mistress of this house, and put a stop to what is becoming disgraceful. . . . Mademoiselle Fortuna and Monsieur de Lussan are . . .

All: Fortuna? Paul! . . . Well! What?

Madame Joubard: I asked the Baron to lead Antoinette away. *The Marquise shrugs her shoulders. But look—See! Judge! They group themselves at the wings, leaving the centre clear—from which appears Fortuna with back to audience, fencing with Paul and retreating after a few passes, they wheel so as to both face the audience.*

Paul: Bravo, Mademoiselle, that last pass was perfect.

Oakhurst interested: Bravo! Keep your guard, Luck.

Marquise with eye glass up applauding. To Madame Joubard: Confess she has an undeniable figure!

Madame Joubard: Undeniable fiddlesticks.

Madame Pomercy reprovingly: Mademoiselle! Paul!

Oakhurst in vain restrained by Boston rushes to Fortuna and seizes her foil: Look, this is the way to parry that thrust. *Fortuna gazes admiringly while he fences a few minutes with Paul, then he remembers himself, bows gravely to Paul. They lay down the foils—Oakhurst returning to Madame Pomercy.*

Oakhurst: Pardon! Old memories are so powerful.

Fortuna throws herself on a sofa, laughing and fanning herself with her handkerchief: How jolly—not bad for a first bout, was it? *To Madame Pomercy.* Don't I do credit to my fencing master? *To Antoinette.* Tony, your turn now. Paul, give a foil to her—she can try her hand with Jack.

Madame Joubard freezingly: Useless, Monsieur de Lussan. Young *ladies* do not fence.

Fortuna consolingly to Antoinette low: Wait till we are alone. We can try some day when we're tired of our other game.

Boston to Oakhurst: This is a little too much of Roaring Camp.

Madame Pomercy a little severely to Fortuna who is chatting with Paul: Fortuna, you have not, I think, seen Colonel Oakhurst.

Fortuna nodding to him: Oh! Haven't I! Dear old Jack.

Madame Pomercy: But he has only this moment arrived.

Fortuna: Bah! Do you think I waited to meet him here with the regulation company manners, when I saw him coming up the road, and could give him a hug alfresco.[26] I'm not that kind of hairpin, am I, Jack?

Oakhurst smiling: It's true. She jumped over a low hedge, and into my arms, just now as I rode up.

Fortuna: And flew back to Paul and the foils.

Marquise to Madame Joubard maliciously: Do you think she meant you by foils?

Boston while others converse taking Fortuna apart: Really you forget, you are not in California, nor even at Mrs. Smith's. You *must* be more on your guard.

Fortuna laughing: Just what Paul says. I forgot to parry. . . . *mimicks fencing.*

Boston impatiently: I do not mean that. Your wild manners expose you to thrusts which may wound as quickly as that shining steel.

Fortuna looking back at others: Wound me? Papa Boston, in good society, don't they always put buttons on their foils?

Madame Joubard to Paul: You look hot and tired after all this romping, which must be so uncongenial to your tastes.

Boston to Fortuna who has heard: Not always, you see.

Paul catches Fortuna's eye and nods kindly to her—she makes a face at Madame Joubard unseen by her. He laughs: Remember that imprudence however guarded by innocence.

Fortuna demurely: Is it not as good as a lone hand?

Boston: You are incorrigible.

Fortuna: I'm thinking of the day of the big fire at San Francisco when we cut off from the rest and ran to it, and you put me on engine No. 6, and the firemen made me an honourary member on the spot[27]—dear me! That was innocence guarded by imprudence! Ah! Ah! *Sighing.* But we weren't as grand then, and so proper! *Others have drawn nearer, and listen—some laugh. Madame Joubard throws up her hands.*

Baron: An independent free born American.

Marquise to Paul: A girl true as steel, pure as gold.

Paul low to her: You think so, Mother, don't you?

Boston: Promise to be a good girl, and I shouldn't wonder if you found on your dressing table . . .

Fortuna in dismay: Not another pearl necklace.

Boston: Yes! But why this consternation?

Fortuna: Well, you see; the one Oakhurst gave me was the duplicate of the one Stumpy sent me at Christmas and they say girls don't wear jewelry here. . . .

Madame Pomercy advancing: Mademoiselle Fortuna, can you spare me your guardian now? *To Boston.* Dear Mr. Adams, help me to persuade the Colonel to stay with us tonight and to give up an engagement he pleads to Mrs. Smith.

Boston: He cannot resist so flattering a command.

Oakhurst: With deep regret I must. No one is more gratified than I am to find Fortuna an inmate of a home where she can learn from example how to become an accomplished woman, but still poor Mrs. Smith was for many years a true and faithful friend to us all. *Fortuna flies at him and kisses him on both cheeks. We parted on good terms some time hence, her husband is away, she is a foreigner in Paris—she would be hurt, if learning I was in France, my first—one of my first calls was not for her—and this is her* at home *evening, I understand.*

Marquise: I like that man.

Oakhurst to Madame Pomercy: Need I tell you that it is a sacrifice?

Madame Pomercy: You almost make me regret having allowed my acquaintance with her to drop.

Boston aside: He is undoing my work.

Madame Pomercy: In any case I keep you both to dinner. It is early yet. Will you look round the conservatories? *To Boston and Oakhurst.* We can talk business and Sierra Mines. *Baron offers his arm to Fortuna who has been whispering to Antoinette. She declines it. Paul advances towards her.*

Madame Pomercy markedly: Paul, will you show the way? *They all disappear through Conservatory doors. Antoinette is about to follow. Fortuna drags her back by the waist.*

Madame Joubard looking back: Antoinette, are you coming?

Fortuna whispering: Say you must practice—*aside*.

Antoinette: Dear Mama, I have to study that Sonata of Beethoven.[28]

Madame Joubard disappearing to Baron: Sweet child, she is always improving herself. *Exits. Fortuna & Antoinette strike a few chords, stop, listen, then coming round the piano, sit on music stand. Fortuna draws a pack of cards from her pocket, opens a large music book on her knees, and deals. Every now and then they fancy they hear a noise & put their hands behind them to strike a chord.*

Fortuna: Now Tony, remember what I taught you.

Antoinette hesitatingly: I go it—alone.

Fortuna: But you can't, you little goose—there are only two of us.

Antoinette: Ah yes. I'll bet you fifty centimes!

Fortuna laughing: Fifty whole centimes. I'll go fifty francs better.

Antoinette dropping her cards: If any one heard you—That's gambling.

Fortuna: Of course it is, simpleton. *Business.*

Antoinette: You must be very rich and very extravagant. *Enter footman with tray and letters. Fortuna takes hers, a large envelope, and puzzles over it. Antoinette reads hers.* Mademoiselle Rosalie's bill for my bonnet. *Regretfully*—twenty-five francs—she said it would be twenty-three. How horrid.

Fortuna: Look at this—*with mock emphasis*—listen. "M" . . . I am M. "The directors of the Sierra Mine beg to inform you that the second and third call are made on your shares payable at the Company's office Rue Lafayette 45." You see a banker's letter. *I* have bought shares.

Antoinette: Girls can't.

Fortuna: Girls can. I have, in a mine, a gold mine, the Sierra mine.

Antoinette picking up the letter: A call! What is a call!?

Fortuna: A call is . . . Well, I don't exactly know. I suppose it's the way the money comes in.

Antoinette reading: Oh! Yes. And what a lot it is. 167,000 francs. *Admiringly.* You are a millionaire.

Fortuna disparagingly: Oh! Those little French francs—they don't go for much.

Antoinette: Mr. Adams got that call for you.

Fortuna: Not much! Don't tell him. I'll show him soon. I am not the rattlebrain he thinks.

Antoinette: But how did you know?

Fortuna: Oh! Through some dear old friends . . . from California.

Antoinette: Gentlemen?

Fortuna: Yes—yes. . . . Dungaree Jack and Sydney Duck.

Antoinette placidly: Chinese gentlemen.

Fortuna: Nonsense. Come, it's your turn to play. There, I've lost. Ar'n't you glad now it was gambling?

Antoinette: We're very wicked, ar'n't we?

Fortuna: Awfully.

Antoinette: But it's much nicer than the Sonata. *Strikes a few spiteful chords.* And yet it seems to want something.

Fortuna: Yes, a man! *Rising.* You're right, I shall go and fetch Paul.

Antoinette: No. No.

Fortuna looking at her: No? Well, have the Baron. He is in the garden — call him.

Antoinette hesitating, business: If I dared. I never could. Besides they would hear me — and then!!!

Fortuna whistling: Yes! Then!! But bless your innocent stupid head, you need not scream out his name. Let me teach you a wrinkle, you simpleminded French baby. Look. *Takes pen & paper, scribbles, & reads.* "Come up and take a hand." *Looks round, sees small ornament on shelf, seizes it, wraps paper round it.*

Antoinette: But that is Madame Pomercy's bronze Mercury.

Fortuna throwing it out of window: Just in his line of business, then. He is sure to pick it up. *Resume their seats.*

Antoinette: Footsteps. There he is. *They go on playing with their backs to the door. Enter Madame Joubard who stops at garden door.*

Fortuna reaching behind her without looking round holds out a hand of cards: There you are.

Madame Joubard: Antoinette! . . . Mademoiselle Del Campo. This is what I shall not allow to pass. *Antoinette very much frightened, tries various ways of hiding her confusion.*

Fortuna waiting: You don't pass! What do you do?

Madame Joubard: My daughter, I order you.

Fortuna interrupting: Tony — she orders you up! We'll euchre her! *The image is thrown back at the window — girls rush to it.*

Madame Joubard seizes it—reads: "Come up and take a hand." *looks round—continues.* "All right, I'm coming." The Marquise, Adèle all must know of this. Antoinette, come, my pure love, follow me. *Drags her away, looking daggers at Fortuna. Exit both.*

Fortuna alone looking after them: Poor Tony. Won't she catch it! *Snaps her fingers.* That for Madame Joubard. I care for none of them save the dear old Marquise and . . .

Paul jumps in at the window, and comes hastily up to Fortuna: Here I am—was Mercury's message meant for me?

Fortuna: You seem to have appropriated it anyhow.

Paul: There was no address and *more seriously* I recognised your handwriting and could not bear that a note from you, however short, should fall in other hands.

Fortuna: That is greedy.

Paul: Tell me—was it meant for me?

Fortuna: Guess.

Paul: For de Trempes perhaps.

Fortuna provokingly: Perhaps—what makes you pitch upon him?

Paul: He followed you about—engrosses you—admires you.

Fortuna: Is that a crime?

Paul: Good Heavens, no! But de Trempes is . . . one of those men . . . confound it, Mademoiselle Fortuna. I cannot speak of the fellow to you.

Fortuna: Poor Baron. I am dying to hear more.

Paul: Pray acquit me of unworthy motives, even if I am jealous.

Fortuna aside: Jealous! *Aloud mockingly.* Why should you be jealous—pray. You are not making love to me, are you?

Paul: You would laugh at me if I did. It is so ridiculous, is it not, to see a man whose whole heart goes forth to a girl, whose thoughts dwell on her night and day—and who would risk his all to dare, and tell her so.

Fortuna more seriously: No girl laughs at what is sincere. *Pause.* If a man felt all you say, he would speak out, like a *man*!

Paul sadly: Not if the woman he loved was rich, very rich, and he was poor—as I am!

Fortuna petulantly: There! Again. Rich! Rich! Ah yes, they may be endowed with gold & property and jewels, the heiresses you speak of, but they must be beggared in heart and soul, for they must live in dread of fortune hunters, and see themselves shunned by honest men, whose pride outweighs their love.

Paul: Fortuna! Fortuna!

Fortuna: In my country we care little who has the money if both have . . . *stops short, turning her head away.*

Paul: Fortuna, I have no pride, or rather, I lay it at your feet, the words rise unbidden to my lips. I love you. I love you!

Fortuna recovering herself after a start: You said just now it was the Baron! *More kindly.* Are you sure? Look at me—the girl who scandalizes your cousin twenty times in one day, who causes the whites of Madame Joubard's eyes to turn up in virtuous horror—the girl who . . .

Paul: Whom my mother loves and respects, Fortuna.

Fortuna: Dear Marquise. God bless her. She is a trump. I love her, too. Paul—pardon. Monsieur Paul! You are not the first who has made love to me, just a bit, to try, for fun, but, but—

Paul: But what?

Fortuna: I laughed them out of it—and we remained friends. But now—Boston was right. I cannot fence with you—the button is off your foil. Somehow you strike *pointing to her heart*—home!

Paul seizing her hand: You bid me hope. Fortuna, say it again!

Fortuna shyly: I thought you had heard and understood. . . . *disengaging her hand.* Have you not?

Paul: You have made me so happy. This very day my mother shall speak to your guardian.

Fortuna surprised: Why, she does not want to marry Jack! Is that the way you do it in France? Ah! I see—*earnestly.* Paul, your friends do not like me—do not go back upon me, do not preach, do not wish me after a while other than I am. I give you fair warning. I am, well, just myself.

Paul: Remain as you are, ever the best, the brightest, the girl I love and swear to protect and guard against the whole world.

Fortuna laughing: Remember also that I have been spoilt by a dozen Fathers, and tremble.

Paul: No dozen Fathers could cherish you as I do, my darling. *Puts his arm round her. Enter Zélie, who seeing them talk low stops at door & watches.*

Zélie aside: I interrupt. What has come to them all? Mademoiselle Antoinette is in the Conservatory with the Baron. Madame in the fernery with the new gentlemen, and now these two. An epidemic of tête à têtes. *Coughing affectedly. Paul starts back guiltily.*

Fortuna quite unconcerned: What is the matter? *Seeing Zélie.* Ah, Zélie, what do you want? Paul, don't go!

Zélie aside: Cool, upon my word. *Aloud.* Visitors for Mademoiselle.

Fortuna impatiently: Bother them. Who is it?

Zélie: Messieurs Smeeth and Skaggs.

Fortuna, with a cry of joy: Stumpy—Skaggs! Impossible.

Zélie: The . . . the persons gave those names. Yes.

Fortuna: They! Here! How jolly. Show them in at once. *Exit Zélie. To Paul.* Oh! This is perfect happiness. Paul, I love them so.

Paul regretfully: I shall leave you to those dear friends. Fortuna, you do not want me now. *Turns towards door.*

Fortuna excitedly: No, No. *Exit Paul—rushes to door—enter Skaggs and Stumpy nearly overturning Zélie. Fortuna embraces them, dances round them.* My dear Stumpy! My dear old nurse.

Zélie: Her nurse. What next. How American. *Exits.*

Stumpy extravagantly showily dressed: Look at her. *To Skaggs.* Ain't she just 2.40 on a shell road.[29] Ain't she nifty. Look at that style. Would ye reckon this was the baby I rocked in a long Tom rocker[30] for a cradle, the little colty girl that jumped from the tail board of Jinny's wagon, when I used to cart dirt from the claim. She's a queen.

Skaggs dressed in black, white tie like a Parson: She's four aces.[31] *They hold her hands, walk round her. Stumpy whispers to Skaggs, sit down rigidly, awkwardly, doing company manners.*

Fortuna laughing: Well! What's up now?

Skaggs solemnly: You see, Miss, it's rather cheeky for two old sardines like us to be fooling round an A-1 first class young lady.

Stumpy approvingly: That's it. A couple of old grizzlies that don't know enough to keep their paws out of a beegum.[32]

Fortuna runs to them, drags them about—business: You dear old donkeys! Drop that! What nonsense! Unlimber yourselves!—Go—and sit down on that sofa—there. *Removes their hats, rubs up their hair—kisses them.* And now wait. *Rings a bell, runs to door, gives an order, draws a low stool between them and sits leaning her head against them and patting their hands.* There. That's something like old times. Isn't it? Do you know what's coming? Some of the best Robinson whiskey,[33] sent me by Kentuck to the Sacré Coeur—three years ago—suppressed by the Superior—*with horror, found afterwards in my boxes, and unpacked . . . with an air. . . . laughs.* You will be the first to taste it.

Skaggs devoutly: Never. Tis a deadly poison.

Fortuna in astonishment: What? You? *You* say that?

Stumpy: Hasn't touched licker for five years, since he had the jimjams,[34] saw the grizzlies walking round with their hair in curl papers, and was a howling lunatic for six months.

Fortuna, shaking her finger at him: Naughty! Shocking!

Stumpy: Now to proceed against it—snatches old soakers bald headed in five minutes. Don't eat any animal food, but lives on yarbs[35] and grass. They call him Professor now!

Skaggs important: Yes! Yes, I may say I'm livin' the new Life!

Fortuna innocently: How queer you must feel! Do you like it? *Enter Butler with tray, decanter, glasses, looks superciliously at the two men, offers the whiskey. Skaggs refuses ostentatiously.*

Stumpy taking some: Well, it ain't my way, Forty, is it, to spoil sport and let good liquor go beggin'? Here's to you, Forty! And may you always keep the comfort you find here in Europe and the love you left behind you in Roaring Camp. . . . I say, boy, *clapping Butler on back.* That's a toast you can drink any day! Join us! Fill up to your young lady, eh? *Butler looks appealingly at Fortuna, who sits and laughs merrily at his embarrassment.*

Skaggs pulling Stumpy aside: You God forsaken ass! Don't you see it's a servant and not a Major General? They don't drink with them sorts here. You'll bring discredit on the Luck.

Butler with dignity, trying to catch Fortuna's eye: Many thanks to Monsieur & Mademoiselle, but I never touch spirits.

Fortuna: May you be forgiven!

Skaggs eagerly: What, you never drink?

Butler impressively: Never!

Skaggs grasping his hand: Give your fist,[36] old bee's wax. Stop! There's a blue ribbon for you. *Places ribbon & badge on butler's coat.* There, you reformed inebriate. You're a full private in the Pacific Legion of the Cold Water Army[37] of which I am Field Marshal. . . . *Exit Butler.*

Fortuna: Well, now we're alone, tell me all about home! *To Stumpy.* You're looking so well. Dear me! Quite a swell. *Stumpy struts round, exhibiting watch &c. &c.* And grown rich, so I hear.

Stumpy: Well, I reckon the sole Proprietor of the Universal Hotel of All Nations in San Francisco,[38] with ten stories, sixteen elevators, eight hundred bedrooms, lit by electricity with a Pullman palace car, direct from New York, landing ye under the *Porte cochére*,[39] ain't in a destitoot condition. Not to say anything about an undivided original two thirds of the Blazing Star mine. Eh! And the best of it all is that a fifth of the income, according to the old agreement, you know, belongs to you.

Fortuna: You are spoiling me, Papa Stumpy. You and Skaggs and the others club together to make me a proud, conceited, stuck up heiress! Fie for shame. And it's horrid to be one! Oh! My darlings, why did you ever strike pay gravel[40] in Roaring Camp?

Stumpy: Look yer, Forty. There ain't some feller hanging round you? I say there ain't some of them fortin' hunting chaps slushing round ye?

Fortuna embarrassed: No. . . . No. . . .

Skaggs: 'Cos you know they've got to get *our* consent first, & if they think of tryin' it on, without why . . . *just shows pistol* . . . darn my skin.

Fortuna hastily: Oh, no—I mean . . . nothing. *Aside.* Will they take kindly to Paul, and Paul to them? *Aloud.* Besides, you know Boston and Oakhurst are both here.

Both interrupting: In Paris?

Fortuna: In this very house, and . . . *They rise abruptly.* You look annoyed. . . . What is it? Are you not friends? Tell me, there is no breach in the old Brotherhood of Roaring Camp?

Stumpy looking for his hat: No. Yes. . . . We must be going.

Skaggs—same business: It's gettin' sort o' late.

Fortuna stopping them: You are keeping something back. For shame! A secret from me, who was always the confidante of the camp. *Stumpy and Skaggs exchange looks, then leading her to a sofa, and sitting down beside her.*

Stumpy: It's ten years since you left Roaring Camp, Forty, and in ten years things change, and men change with them. Why, Lord bless you, Forty, Roaring Camp ain't Roaring Camp no longer. It's called Chry-so-po-lis, and boys there wear a biled shirt everyday. It ain't no more pardners together, bunkers in the same cabin, wet & dry season, in luck & out o' luck. Some men try different ways, and them who had the same ways hez drifted off together. Some hez found new friends ez nat'ral ez quicksilver takes up with gold. Now there's Boston and Oakhurst, they're rich, jabber French and Eyetalian, and Latin, they've got a gilt-edged swaller tailed style[41] and they're at home where everything is gilt-edged and swaller tailed and fancy fixings. We—that's me and Skaggs, and Sydney Duck and Dungaree Jack, kin only run alongside o' ye, but somehow we can't ketch on! We ain't got the gait. And we ain't going to let them make you ashamed of Roaring Camp.

Fortuna starting: I ashamed! Who dares say this? Who dares say you are not good enough for them? For me?

Skaggs looking round: It's been kinder dropped round promiskus like that we ain't to show hands in this yer game, but to pass out. We are expected to give the go-by to Roaring Camp when ever any of them gilt-edged swaller tails is about. Some of your other fathers think we stand in your way by bringing up old times, and so we've concluded to come over here jest to say "God bless you, Luck" once more and then drop out o' this crowd forever. *Moves to go.*

Fortuna standing before door with crossed arms: Do you think I shall let you leave me like this? No! No!—*Comes forward between them.* Listen to me. You shall confront Boston, Oakhurst, and my new friends—now. You shall see which of them dare dictate how much of my past life I must forget at their bidding! *Mute protestation of the men.* I have not done. They dine here today. So shall you! As honoured guests as they are! Or—or—I shall go! Will that satisfy you? *Moves to bell.*

Stumpy arresting her hand on bell: Let them go, Luck! Let them go! Lord love you, dear! say that again, stand up for your old fathers like that and we'll cut everything, Roaring Camp, Blazing Star, Boston, Oakhurst, and the whole caboodle![42] There! Then! *Fortuna sobs.*

Skaggs: You predestined old ass! You've made her cry. Don't mind him, Luck. We thank you for invitin' us, but we can't stay—we never meant to stay. We're too proud to give them chaps a chance to laugh at us. But what that old fool was trying to get off was this. He hasn't seen his wife yet—he wanted a sight of your blessed face as soon as ever he set foot in Paris. He must look her up now . . . and Kentuck. . . .

Stumpy interrupting him: Yes, yes—my wife!

Fortuna eagerly: Kentuck! What! Is he in Paris, too?

Stumpy hastily: No!

Skaggs hesitatingly: Yes . . . yes . . . that is . . . he was . . . I think.

Fortuna: And well? And happy? Dear Kentuck!

Stumpy nudging Skaggs: Well? Happy? Ye . . . es.

Fortuna: Why have you not brought him? Does he also think me proud and fine?

Stumpy taking her hand embarrassed: No, my child, no. But you see, Forty, we've heard he's been a little down in his luck. It was his way, you remember . . . *laughing affectedly* and he didn't *care to let you know* — ha! Ha! *Hurriedly.* But time's up. *To Skaggs.* Come along, old Pard. Good bye.

Fortuna kissing them. Business: No! No! Not yet. Well! It is not goodbye anyhow but "Au revoir."

Skaggs: That's as you like, Forty dear. O'er the river — or anywhere. *Business — both exit.*

Fortuna alone looking after them: Dear old tender hearted idiots! I'd like to knock their foolish heads together. Not good enough for me — or anyone — Nonsense — the truest — the best. Poor Skaggs, that white tie does not suit his style of beauty. I must tell him so next time, and get at the bottom of this ridiculous pet against Jack and Boston. And I am sure there is a mystery about Kentuck. They tried to put me off and I let them think they had — but I intend to make Oakhurst find out all about it! I shall not rest till I've brought the old Brotherhood together again!

Paul entering with flowers, aside: They have gone! *Aloud.* Fortuna, I bring you some roses. Wear them tonight.

Fortuna taking them heedlessly: Thanks. *Suddenly.* Paul! You like Adams, don't you?

Paul surprised: Yes!

Fortuna: And Oakhurst?

Paul warmly: Immensely. So does my mother — it is to him she will speak at the first opportunity *fondly* and ask him for his ward. He is a perfect *gentleman*.

Fortuna a little impatiently: And . . . Mrs. Smith?

Paul more reservedly: Yes. . . . Oh yes. . . . Mrs. Smith loves you — that is enough for me.

Fortuna eagerly: That is so, is it not? You will care for all those I love — who love me. . . . You will stand by them.

Paul: Certainly.

Fortuna warningly: Always, Paul. For my sake?

Paul: Always! *Kisses her hands. They move aside.*

Marquise entering with Madame Joubard: Well, here are two of them already. *Aside* a pretty group—and here comes my niece. Now for your indictment.

Madame Pomercy entering to Fortuna: Fortuna! Fortuna!—*She comes forward.* Tonight is the *at home* of your old friend & chaperone Mrs. Smith. It has been proposed that we should all take this opportunity of paying off old arrears of civility, and go there en masse. Colonel Oakhurst takes the responsibility of this invasion.

Fortuna clapping her hands: Delightful. Thank you, Madame! *Aside.* How *this* will bring them all together.

Marquise: I am perfectly willing. *Aside* The taboo'd Mrs. Smith, the great interdicted. *To Madame Pomercy aside.* The irresistible Colonel has lost no time in carrying the first bulwarks of the citadel.

Madame Pomercy: Dear Aunt! For Fortuna's sake I must go!

Madame Joubard primly: I do not for one moment contemplate taking Antoinette there. I would cut that woman!

Fortuna springing forward: You!

Marquise restraining her gently—to Madame Pomercy: Adèle. . . . *Significantly.* De Trempes comes with us, of course?

Madame Pomercy: Oh yes! He is delighted.

Marquise to Madame Joubard: We shall take your excuses. . . . You will find the evening dull here alone, dear Madame Joubard!

Madame Joubard: Well, no. I change my mind. Mrs. Smith might be hurt. Those sort of people are very sensitive to a slight from us. We shall go. Antoinette must keep to her own set. . . .

Marquise: You are consideration itself. *To Paul aside.* That woman is the goddess of inconsistency.

Paul wearily: So she is—but she should be gagged.

Madame Joubard: One moment. I have a painful duty to perform—one which as a mother I dare not shrink from, lest the evil consequences which might ensue should be charged on my part to too great leniency.

Marquise: Oh! Never that.

Madame Joubard: Adèle, it is *your* duty, and your right to warn Mademoiselle del Campo against carrying on clandestine correspondence with men unknown. . . .

Paul furious: Madame Joubard, take care of what you say—

Fortuna angrily: What does the woman mean?

Madame Pomercy: Hush! Explain yourself.

Madame Joubard viciously producing paper and statuette: This invitation was thrown out of the window to a man who expected it, for he shortly sent back an answer—the same medium—it fell at my feet—here it is—Mademoiselle del Campo's writing, perfectly plain—the man's, not so plain. What the hidden significance of the statuette is, I am not prepared to explain. See and judge.

Fortuna bursts out laughing: Paul, *you* answered it. *Insisting,* say so. Come.

Madame Joubard triumphantly: She owns it.

Madame Pomercy: Fortuna, did you do this?

Fortuna defiantly: It looks like it, doesn't it?

Madame Pomercy: You wrote to Paul.

Fortuna shrugging her shoulders: He took for himself anyhow.

Madame Pomercy: You must be more careful, Mademoiselle Fortuna—in our world such . . . indiscretion, to call it by a harsher name—is not allowed.

Paul interposing: Dear Adèle—a joke—a mere nothing—pray say no more about it.

Fortuna: Mr. Paul. Pray do not apologize for me. *Aside to him.* You don't think it wrong?

Paul: Oh! No—of course not.

Madame Pomercy: No man tells a pretty girl to her face that she has been indiscreet. . . . But enough of this—there is the first dinner bell. Remember, ladies, we leave for Paris immediately on rising from table. *To Fortuna.* No injudicious display of jewelry. Pray . . . Paul, a word with you. *Paul at the door looks back at Fortuna who is looking at him—she slowly takes up the roses & kisses them, then remains abstracted, the Marquise watching her—exits with Paul & Madame Joubard.*

Marquise to Fortuna who stands abstracted: My child. Do not fret. Be patient & good. Come, come—wear white tonight. *Kissing her.* Paul likes it.

Fortuna: Oh, Madame, why am I always blamed, always criticised.

Marquise smiling: Because—because we would give our little finger to be like you . . . and can't. . . . *exits.*

Fortuna alone. Night is coming on, the stage gradually darkens—she goes and sits near table. After a pause: Ah well! They are a strange lot. I cannot make them out. But Paul knows it was only a joke—a harmless silly joke—For his sake I will be careful—& prim—& proper—not for theirs—*defiantly*—No, not for theirs. I wonder if it is true that men never tell the truth to women—flatter them, and then go back upon them. Good Heavens, I should believe no harm of Paul—not if I saw him do the most unlikely thing—I would just go up to him, put my hand in his, look into his eyes and say, Paul, tell me what it means? *Starting* What is that? *Listening. Footsteps on the gravel. Goes to glass door and looks out.* A man lurking behind the bushes—afraid to be seen—he is making for this room—I must give the alarm. No, I am not a frightened timid French Demoiselle.[43] I can help myself. I'll show them how the Luck of Roaring Camp behaves—*rushes out.*

Kentuck entering cautiously at glass door: Gone! She was here a minute ago. I saw her from out there, in all her beauty and war paints and features—alone. Gone, and with her the only chance I had to speak to her once more, the chance I have watched for these two hours. There was a door here—behind this curtain. *Goes towards it.*

Fortuna throwing curtain aside, pointing pistol: Halt! Another step and I fire!

Kentuck starts, then with extravagant satisfaction: It's her! The identical attitude! The very position I taught her. Straight & stiff as a ramrod from her waist, the hand in a line with her eye. *Throws his hat in the air.* She's got me covered, the d—d little cuss!

Fortuna: Throw up your hands!

Kentuck: Not until you've shaken them, Forty.

Fortuna throwing down pistol & flying to his arms: Kentuck! Ah! If I had killed you! *Looking at him.* But why this disguise?

Kentuck: Disguise! . . . Ah yes—it's a disguise . . . certainly.

Fortuna: You look thin & ill.

Kentuck: I'm better now. Ah! Luck, the sight of your dear face is better than medicine or food. *Seems ready to drop.*

Fortuna leading him to chair: Good God! You frighten me! You are not faint, are you? Kentuck, dear Kentuck, what is the matter? *Kneeling by him.* Are you in trouble? In pain? Speak, father! I will be your nurse. Are you in want? I have money to spare. What is it?

Kentuck recovering himself: Nothing, child, nothing. I'm an old fool. I was always that, you know. I oughtn't to have come—that's all.

Fortuna rising aside: Something is kept from me that I must & shall know. *Aloud* I'm no longer a child. You must talk to me as to a woman who can comfort you—even assist you.

Kentuck aside: She is right. *Aloud.* Listen, Forty. A year ago it seemed as if my sorter luck was lifting for two old pards. *Hastily.* You don't know them, Forty—no, no. Two friends offered to let me into a big mine of theirs they were taking to Europe.[44] They wanted me, because maybe you remember, child, there was no man in Californy whose word was as good ez to the value of a mine. I didn't care a cuss about the money nor the shares, but it gave me a chance of once more seeing my little girl, and being near her—I accepted—I came over a week ago. The very night after I arrived the police arrested Syd . . . my friends, who had only time to send me a warning to keep away—and nabbed my papers.

Fortuna: Arrest your friends. For what?

Kentuck: That's just what gets me. It seems that yer mine turned out to be no mine at all, but the biggest kind of a bluff, and in this yer Godforsaken country they call it a crime. Why, Lord love you, Forty, if that had been the fashion in California, half the population would have been in jail. I reckon it was because a lot o' swell got into it—at least I've heard there's one that is a nobleman.

Fortuna: And these wretches—your friends!

Kentuck aside: It's luck I didn't let out it was Sydney Duck & Dungaree Jack, her fathers. *Aloud.* Well, you see, they've got away since.

Fortuna: You must see Oakhurst at once—he's here—he can clear you.

Kentuck: I! Stand up before him—as I am—in these rags! Never!

Fortuna: What's to be done, then? *Aside.* I have it—Yes! Stumpy. *Aloud.* Listen, dear Kentuck. I am going to Mrs. Stumpy—Mrs. Smith, 35 Champs Elysses—you know—tonight. Come there late and make it your refuge.

Kentuck angrily: Mrs. Stumpy—her carriage wheels spattered me on the Bullyvards last night. Give her a chance of flouting my shame, and my rags—no—no!

Fortuna: Oh! You are unfair to her! Believe me. *Kentuck shakes his head. Imploringly.* But Stumpy, your old friend Stumpy—

Kentuck: He's four thousand miles away.

Fortuna joyfully: No. He is here! In Paris. He arrived this morning.

Kentuck bitterly: And did not look me up. *Aside* So! He has heard all.

Fortuna hurriedly: Nonsense! How could he find you when the police can't—luckily. *Coaxingly. Baron enters suddenly, starts on observing Fortuna & Kentuck.*

Baron aside: A tête-à-tête—but not Paul! I must watch. *Withdraws in door way.*

Kentuck: I thought I heard steps, listen. *Draws pistol from pocket.*

Fortuna: Put up your weapon, dear. You have no enemies here. If any body were to enter here I should boldly proclaim you my father—one of the best & truest of Roaring Camp!

Kentuck: No! Never! I should only shame you in these rags.

Fortuna: Come, then, to my room—you are safer there—and I'll find you a disguise to throw over them. *Aside.* I'll rummage Paul's wardrobe, and won't he be surprised when he finds it out. Such fun! *Aloud* Come! *Exit with Kentuck.*

Baron: So. I thought to steal an interview with my charmer, and find her tête-à-tête with one of those wild ruffianly fathers of hers. An old man from his voice. I could not see his face. What a prospect for a son-in-law? Well, it might have been worse—for a moment I thought it was Paul himself. Paul! Paul! Eh! Why should he not taste the sweets of jealousy—& see his charmer with the man. He is proud—impulsive—haughty! it would be enough to break their engagement. I'll do it—*Exit.*

Fortuna entering laughing: I've rigged out the dear old boy with Paul's hat & riding boots, & this cloak—*pushing one up from wing*—will quite transform him. How Paul will laugh over this when Kentuck is safe & cleared, & I can tell him the whole story. *Reenters with cloak on her arm Left. Enter cautiously Baron leading Paul by the hand.*

Paul: There is no one here—you must have been mistaken. No thief would venture here at this hour.

Baron: I saw a man as plainly as I see you. See, the window is open. He may have passed out here on the verandah. Whose room is that beyond?

Paul: Mademoiselle Fortuna—she must be dressing. *Anxiously.* Good Heavens, he would not have . . . *Darts forward, held back by Baron.*

Baron: Silence—hush—voices. *Withdraws with Paul in curtained recess—as door Left opens Fortuna enters leading Kentuck closely muffled.*

Baron *low with affected surprise:* Mademoiselle del Campo.

Paul: Fortuna. Good God.

Fortuna *going towards balcony:* Good night! Not for long. Hush, don't speak—you will not be heard or seen. . . . *Kisses him, coaxingly.* Go now, darling, and expect me in two hours. *Lovingly.* Stay. I'll take you myself through the shrubbery. *Exits with Kentuck's arm round her. Paul has during this time shown great emotion—nearly rushing forward, then restraining himself. Baron, shrugging his shoulders, is about to look out after them, when Paul with sudden resolution holds him back, closes the window, draws the curtains, turns up the lamps & comes forward gravely.*

Paul: Monsieur de Trempes, you are a man of the world. I do not ask your opinion of what you have seen tonight. *With an effort.* I neither explain or defend it. But you are a gentleman also, Baron, therefore I need not tell you what is our duty.

Baron: Perfectly. Madame Pomercy should be warned to what consequences her indiscriminate hospitality exposes her.

Paul: You will not do that.

Baron: And why not?

Paul: Because it would involve me in the disagreeable necessity of calling the man who gave such warning a spy, a liar, and a coward.

Baron: Monsieur de Lussan!

Paul coolly: A spy, because suspecting a young girl, he brought me here to witness a clandestine meeting. A liar, because I shall deny upon my honour as a French officer any story that could compromise a woman. A coward, if he suffers me to proceed without at once demanding satisfaction.

Baron aside: A fight—he the avenger, I, the accuser—no—no—Monsieur Paul.

Paul: I am waiting, Baron, to hear what you decide.

Baron with affected cheerfulness: My good fellow. I was simply trying you—no, of course, I shall be silent as the tomb. There's my hand. . . . *Paul takes it coolly. Aside* If the little heiress turns restive, I've got the whip hand now. *At door.* Silent as the tomb . . . ha! Ha . . . *Exits laughing.*

Paul alone sits down dejectedly: And so ends my short dream. I was to her—only a blind—a tool. That note I picked up was not meant for me, but for *that* . . . man. . . . He came at her bidding. Who could have thought her capable of such duplicity. Her words of tenderness lied—her rippling laughter lied—her sweet tremulous lips lied. It is too cruel. Ah Fortuna, Fortuna, why did I ever see you? Can I forget you? Will my contempt even kill my love? *Hides his face in his arms.*

Marquise entering: One word only before they all join us. *Comes up to him.* Good news, Paul. I have seen the Colonel—you are an accepted suitor, if his ward consents. *Playfully.* Little doubt of that, eh?

Paul starting: Oh Mother! Why did you do that?

Marquise: To hasten your happiness, & serve your impatience.

Paul bitterly: My happiness! I have changed my mind. I shall not marry. For . . . Mademoiselle del Campo . . .

Marquise: Are you mad? My word is engaged.

Paul: It matters not. She does not love me.

Marquise reassured laughing: I see. A lover's quarrel. Oh! You big baby.

Paul seriously: No, Mother—no passing misunderstanding. Take my word, we are parted forever.

Marquise: A long word at twenty-four! No rash vows—*changing her tone*—But you suffer? What is it? Explain.

Paul: There is nothing to explain. I neither blame nor complain. I am only quite sure that this marriage can never be.

Marquise impatiently: Sure—nonsense—sure—men never can be sure. Your future is linked with Fortuna's now.

Paul: She is free—now.

Marquise: Paul! You fancy you know something against her. *Movement to Paul.* Oh! I know my son well enough not to ask him to lift his voice against any girl—but your mother sees, poor boy, that you have condemned her in your heart. Remember that before accusing a woman you must have proofs—overwhelming proofs—and even then don't believe them.

Paul: Hush! Here she comes. *Enter Fortuna. Marquise watches her intently.*

Fortuna looking confused. Aside: Caught. *Comes forward—as all the others enter in evening dress—Oakhurst, Boston, Madame Pomercy, Madame Joubard, Antoinette, Baron.*

Baron pursuing conversation very fussily: Quite a false alarm, dear ladies, I assure you—some blunder of the servants, some harmless beggar got lost in the grounds. *Fortuna bends forward anxiously. Paul looks at her.* Alms were thrown at him, presumably from this window—my groom saw him leaving the avenue....

Fortuna drawing back aside: It's all right now.

Baron to Paul: Silent as the tomb, you see. *Paul presses his hand.*

Madame Joubard: Your presence of mind in peril is invaluable, Baron.

Antoinette: We might have been murdered in our beds.

Marquise dryly: Hardly! Just before dinner! *The gong sounds.*

Madame Pomercy: Dinner! We will abstain from all ceremonials. Colonel! *Takes Oakhurst's arm—Boston pairs with Madame Joubard—making a wry face at Fortuna who laughs at him—and then turns to Paul.*

Fortuna: Not dressed yet! You see—but I shall wear your roses, never fear.

Paul starting, then coldly: They will be withered then, Mademoiselle. *Fortuna stares at him and is about to take his arm playfully, when bowing to her, he turns to Marquise.* Mother! *They move on together.*

Madame Joubard at door: Monsieur de Trempes. Antoinette is awaiting you.

Fortuna alone in middle of stage, looking dazed, then suddenly clapping her hands: Bless him! He's playing at quarrelling—what fun!

Curtain.

Act II

Mrs. Smith's/Stumpy's house in the Champs Elysées, Paris. Drawing room gorgeously furnished, in contrast with elegant simplicity of the Villa Pomercy. Folding doors leading to vestibule in Center. On Left arch with portière leading to other rooms, which are visible. On Right two more doors, fireplace. Powdered footmen lighting sconces. Preparations for a party.

Marie arranging flowers: That will do now. *Exit footmen.* The same thing over and over again. Dinners, parties, concerts, and Madame never knowing who is coming, whom she has asked, and *looking at clock* never ready to receive her guests. It's scandalous, an old woman like her. *Sits down and fingers papers, bones, jewel cases*—for she *is* old spite her wigs, her rouge, and her juvenile toilettes. A widow, who probably killed her husband with grief, if ever there was a Monsieur Smeeth. Humph! *Looking at herself in the glass.* I did think she had managed to hook Monsieur de Trempes, but when Mademoiselle Fortuna came from school, he made eyes at *her*—and now she's gone he's very scarce—so is M. de Lussan—at last! we have plenty more—men, I mean, not so many ladies. *Opening envelopes.* Let's see today's bills. "Worth," a fancy dress.[45] Folly, hardly a disguise that. *Skims bills.* Total 5,560 fr. Pouh! Bysderfeld *laughs* one black curly wig—one virgin gold toupet and curls—hare's foot and Blanc de Perle-Rouge[46] for veins. 1,500 fr. *Looking at clock.* The hair dresser is still with her and it is nearly ten. Ah! A telegram! Unopened. The same I gave Madame this morning when she went to the races. The giddy old thing.

Opens it. "Expect me this evening. Just landed. William Henry." Well, Monsieur William Henry is in luck, whoever he is, for he might have found the lady flown, instead of hitting on a gala night. *Starts.* The hall bell. I knew it! The guests and she still painting and titivating. *Stumpy entering with Skaggs. Marie drops curtsy, is not noticed and stands wondering.*

Stumpy *to footmen without*: All right. I'll find my way. *To Skaggs, looking round.* Not bad? Eh? Not just up to the new bridal suite in the Universal Hotel, Frisco, but pretty decent for Paris. Eh! The old gal has not stinted herself.

Marie *aside*: What singular men! Never saw quite as bad as that here before. I shan't leave them alone, anyhow.

Stumpy *who has examined furniture*: I reckon that sofy alone cost nigh unto a thousand as it stands.

Skaggs *mournfully*: Extravagance! Willful extravagance. It would have bought her father's farm years ago.

Stumpy *seeing Marie*: Hallo! How do you do? *Offers hand. Marie drops curtsy.* The chambermaid, I reckon.

Marie: The lady's maid of Madame.

Stumpy: Ah, I see. You couldn't about tell me what that sofy cost?

Marie *aside*: Are they bailiffs? *Aloud* I don't fancy Madame knows.

Skaggs: Of course not. And I can remember when she knew to a cent the price of pork.

Stumpy *to Marie*: Hold on a moment, here. *To Skaggs.* Get the girl to give you a drink while I hunt up Frances Jane. Where is she? *To Marie. Looks round.*

Marie *aside*: William Henry perhaps. *Frigidly* If Monsieur means Madame, Monsieur Bysderfeld is with her in her bedroom and she cannot be disturbed. *Both men stare at each other in comic horror.*

Stumpy: Monsieur? Who?

Marie: The hairdresser! *Stumpy relieved tries different doors and is severely told by Marie he cannot enter. Business.*

Stumpy: What's the number of her room?

Skaggs: Don't be a fool. This isn't a hotel.

Stumpy: That's what they call French houses here.

Marie aside: Can it be a tradesman with a bill? *Aloud.* You can't see Madame at this hour. It is impossible.

Skaggs: Don't insist, you all! It ain't the French style for wives to see their husbands except in public.

Stumpy philosophically: Oh, I can wait. No hurry. *To Skaggs looking at Marie.* I say, she'd just fill the bill as an imported American chambermaid, with a little more jewelry and ribbons. *To Marie.* See here, Mary Ann.

Marie: Pardon. Marie.

Stumpy: I said to—Marie. *Sits down. Points to chair and lolls on sofa.* What does your mistress pay you?

Marie: Eighty francs a month, Monsieur! And perquisites. *Aside.* Plenty of them.

Stumpy: I'll make it dollars. *Marie perplexed.* Four hundred francs.

Marie: Monsieur!

Stumpy: I'll get some one to fill your place here, and you'll go back with me to San Francisco. You needn't say anything to Madame about it.

Marie indignant: Oh, won't I though! At once too. *Aside.* The old reprobate! *Exits furious.*

Stumpy calling back: Halloo. I say. What the devil. Oh, look yer, Skaggs, you don't reckon she thought—you know . . . that I meant? . . .

Skaggs: Nat'rally, she did. . . .

Stumpy: No wonder she flounced away. She felt insulted.

Skaggs: At the price!!

Stumpy: Oh, I hope she won't blurt out to Frances Jane. I shall have to set it right . . . no . . . I won't. *Musing.* But after all she hasn't set us on the trail of my wife.

Skaggs: Are you sure you have not made another God forsaken blunder? You are not expected.

Stumpy: On the contrary. She's been preparing things, inviting lots of people to meet me. Can't you see? At such times it pays to be out of Frances Jane's way. *Enter Servant ushering in Madame Joubard, Baron, and Antoinette. They look round seeking the lady of the house. Skaggs and Stumpy draw near to each other.*

Baron to Madame Joubard: We are not the first, you see. Although we are early our fine hostess is not over punctual. *Converse with Madame Joubard and Antoinette, moving towards Left.*

Stumpy to Skaggs: I reckon this gilt-edged lot is my wife's company. I suppose I ought to introduce myself and make things sorter pleasant, eh?

Skaggs: No, introduction ain't the style out yer. Besides, you're the master of the house, and in tiptop society the master of the house is the last person you're expected to know.

Madame Joubard to Baron: You are sure, Baron, that Mrs. Smith receives?

Baron: Oh, the very best people . . . French and foreign.

Antoinette: Shall we have dancing?

Stumpy to Skaggs: Then you think I'd better sail in permiskus, eh? *Settles his cuffs and hair.*

Skaggs: Yes! I'll show you the way. *They come forward and meet Baron and ladies with elaborate bows — cold and distant return from all three, who move away and examine pictures.*

Madame Joubard: Good painting. *Aside to Baron.* Who are they?

Baron same: Ah! Ah! Wealthy American railway conductors. *Aside* Cads.

Antoinette affectedly: Baron de Trempes, is this really a good picture?

Stumpy interposing: Yes, Miss. It's about ez good of its kind ez there was in the market. *Points out beauties.*

Madame Joubard aside: Original looking man. Smitten with Tony. *Aloud affectedly.* One of the Old Masters.

Stumpy: No, Ma'am. dear, no. Mine. Mary Frances sent me the bill.

Baron laughing: Very good. Very good. *Aside* Vulgar beast. *Stumpy leads Antoinette to other pictures.*

Madame Joubard to Baron: These American magnates place themselves above the trammels of our civilization. Here this ease and sanguine would be termed bad form. I appreciate it. Yet is it safe to let him engross my daughter. *Aside* I must give Antoinette a chance with de Trempes. *Aloud* Pray join them. *She approaches Skaggs.*

Stumpy to Baron: I say, I don't know your name, you know, but if you like to take a cocktail before the rest o' the crowd come in, why, I'm your man. Nominate your poison.

Antoinette to Baron: Poison! Oh, pray don't think of it. It's one of those dreadful things with a straw Fortuna raves about. *Baron declines in dumb show and sits with Antoinette on a sofa. Stumpy standing before them.*

Madame Joubard confidential and smirking with Skaggs—embarrassed for a subject: Your friend . . . your intelligent compatriot is . . .

Skaggs: He's an ass! But I reckon you're thinking with me, Ma'am, that this yer frivolity and extravagance don't pay. No. Look at the gilt frame & them mirrors. You can't see yourself any the better for them, can you?

Madame Joubard aside: Practical like all his nation. *Aloud sympathisingly* Scarcely. I agree with you.

Skaggs getting bold: And when a woman like yourself looks in one, they don't want a better frame.

Madame Joubard aside: Appreciative very!

Skaggs: It's more than brass.

Madame Joubard: Sir!

Skaggs aside: What in thunder am I saying. *Aloud*. Gold, Madam! 18 carat gold! *Madame Joubard relents, takes his arm and leads him to opposite side.*

Stumpy to Baron and Antoinette who have tried to avoid him, and opened albums, etc: Oh, make yourselves quite at home. Don't mind Mrs. Stumpy Smith. I'm running this hotel.

Antoinette: What does that mean?

Baron: Well. Whatever one pleases. *Aside* Whatever it does mean, he may be useful to me. *Aloud more cordially* Really, my dear Monsieur . . . Monsieur . . .

Stumpy: Smith. William Henry Smith. *Talks to Antoinette.*

Baron aside: The husband, by Jove! Dropped from the clouds. One of Fortuna's fathers. I need to make intersect with all at this juncture. No one seems to recognise him. I shall make the running. *To Antoinette.* Your mother is, I believe, beckoning to you. *Antoinette runs to her mother, who in dumb show reproves her for leaving Baron's side. To Stumpy.* My dear Mr. Smith, delighted to make your acquaintance. On looking at these evidences of perfect taste, we congratulate Mrs. Smith, we envy you.

Stumpy slapping him on the back: If you want a sip, you know . . . eh?

Baron wincing: Nothing could give me great pleasure, but . . . just now . . .

Madame Joubard imperiously: Baron de Trempes!

Baron: You see . . . as a man of the world, you know that I must sacrifice myself. Au revoir. *Joins the ladies.*

Stumpy: Not a bad sort o' chap, after all. Another appointment over the river. Baron Trumpy! Now that's my style of a nobleman. I wish Forty was livin' here. I'd introduce him. She'd fancy him. *Rejoins Skaggs.*

Madame Joubard to Baron: I have found my companion most intelligent. Tell me his name and—*stops* . . . What is his particular railway?

Stumpy to Skaggs: I say, who's the old one? *Pointing to Madame Joubard.*

Skaggs: A sensible woman, who despises extravagance and recognises common sense.

Stumpy: How she must look down on them bracelets of hers.

Skaggs: And who's your friend?

Stumpy airily: He! A Baron of course. Baron Trumpy! *Enter Servant announcing,* "Marquise de Lussan." "Madame Pomercy." "Monsieur de Lussan."

Stumpy to Skaggs: What! More o' them! The whole noblesse oblige of Paris.[47] I say, Frances Jane is going it. You collar the Madame Pomercy and I'll tackle the Markees. I'm more used to titter. *Marquise and Madame Pomercy have joined Madame Joubard. Paul nods to Baron and stands apart.*

Marquise: How is this? Where are the others?

Madame Pomercy: I see neither Adams or the Colonel.

Madame Joubard: Fortuna went, as you know, with her guardians, and we got here first some time since. They cannot be long now.

Madame Pomercy looking round: I am almost sorry I came at all.

Marquise: Not I. There will be a *défilé*[48] of oddities, judging by these specimens. *Aside.* And Madame Joubard must not be allowed to suppose that her malignity has affected Paul. *Stumpy approaches Marquise who quietly ignores him. Madame Pomercy equally snubs Skaggs.*

Stumpy offering seat to Marquise: How do? Is there anything I can do? Say the word.

Marquise quietly dignified: Give orders to my coachman to wait—and hand me a footstool.

Stumpy: Certainly. I say, Skaggs, the Markee's carriage can wait. All right, Ma'am. We'll take the best care of it, won't we, Skaggs?

Marquise to Madame Joubard: Have these men been here long?

Madame Joubard: We found them here. What do you think of them?

Marquise surprised: Think? Does one think about such creatures?

Madame Joubard taken aback: Oh . . . of course not. *At once becomes proud and forbidding to Skaggs and Stumpy.*

Madame Pomercy to Paul: Something must have happened to Col . . . to Fortuna, Paul. *Paul talks to her. She looks distraught.*

Skaggs: Looking for something, Ma'am?

Madame Pomercy coldly: No. Nothing. . . . Yes, open the window. It is insufferably close.

Skaggs: Yes, Ma'am. *To Stumpy.* Stand further off. She says you're insufferably close, and wants you to open the window.

Stumpy: Can't she get out of the door? *Opens window savagely.* There. Anything else, Ma'am?

Madame Pomercy without looking: Nothing, but inform your mistress.

Stumpy: My . . . Eh. What? *Dragging Skaggs aside.* I say, she wants my mistress!

Skaggs: Oh! Oh! *Musing.* Mistress?

Stumpy dejectedly: Mistress!

Skaggs airily: Oh yes! . . . It is their loose and fast French style. Judge others by themselves. Don't seem to mind, and tell her she's coming.

Stumpy: But think of Frances Jane!

Mrs. Stumpy entering noisily—overdressed in would-be juvenile style—eyeglass in eye: A thousand pardons! Could not fly through my toilette quicker. Ah, the dear Marquise. *Rushes to her.*

Stumpy to Skaggs: Another o' them. What a stunner! And not a husband between them.

Skaggs: Not much! A painted Jezebel![49]

Stumpy recognising her: Good Heavens! My wife. *Rushes forward.*

Skaggs detaining him: Watch her a bit, till you've found out her new bearings. *They retire behind the piano.*

Mrs. Stumpy affectedly: A delightful surprise indeed. *To Antoinette, patting her cheek.* You will get lots of beaus here tonight. It is my gala evening. *To Madame Joubard.* You can pick out a husband for her. *To Madame Pomercy.* You have not brought Fortuna. Very wicked of you.

Madame Pomercy: Fortuna is . . .

Mrs. Stumpy interrupting: Oh, I know. You're making her dreadfully goody, goody. Renouncing the world, its pomps, et cetera.

Marquise smiling: Only showing her another side of it, Madame, and turning her a little.

Mrs. Stumpy noticing Baron: Baron! *He offers to kiss her hand coquettishly.* No! No! You monster, I won't shake hands with you. I abhor you. You've quite deserted my Hôtel. Mauvais sujet![50] *To Madame Pomercy.* You have taken him away from me, you wicked, wicked woman.

Madame Pomercy icily: De Trempes, pray assure Mrs. Smith that I do not presume to enter the lists with . . . her . . . for . . . you!

Baron: Dear Mrs. Smith, what must I do to be forgiven? *Lowering tone.* I have been recruiting for your *at home.* See! Rank, beauty, youth, all doing homage at your shrine.

Mrs. Stumpy tapping him with her fan: Go along with you! *To Paul using eyeglass affectedly.* Ah, is this Paul? Little Paul! Another deserter. Oh, don't apologize. I excuse *you*. We know who the attraction was in my house. *Moves off with him.*

Skaggs to Stumpy: She somehow riles me, with *my* house, *my* hotel!

Stumpy: She just strikes me dumb.

Paul to Mrs. Stumpy: I am not ungrateful for your kindness to me.

Mrs. Stumpy: Look you! Paul, there's just as good fish in the water as out of it. I expect lots of pretty girls tonight.

Madame Pomercy to Marquise: She is much worse than she used to be. *Aside.* And Oakhurst not here yet.

Marquise: Never mind. Fancy yourself at a Cafe Chantant.[51] *Movement of Madame Pomercy.* Oh, for once! You need not come again. *Paul joins them.*

Baron to Mrs. Stumpy: I have had the immense gratification of making your husband's acquaintance.

Stumpy nudging Skaggs: Faithful Trumpy. He remembers me.

Skaggs: It's more than she does.

Mrs. Stumpy adjusting her curls, carelessly: Ah indeed! Hope he is well, poor fellow. Didn't know you had ever been to America. *With sudden animation.* Were you at the races this afternoon?

Baron: Dear Mrs. Smith. Not in America—nearer home.

Mrs. Stumpy: Of course, at Longchamp.[52] Rather dull, eh?

Stumpy: Dull! I'll pay her out for that.

Baron: The excellent Monsieur Smith . . . *Fortuna bursts in with hood and opera cloak, nodding all round. Paul withdraws back of stage with Baron and tries not to be seen by Fortuna, who kisses Mrs. Stumpy on both cheeks.*

Fortuna: Well, aunty, that's me! Did you think you'd never see me again? *To Madame Pomercy.* Oh, Madame, Jack—I mean

Oakhurst was awfully sorry not to be here first. But he won't be long now. *Removes wraps.*

Mrs. Stumpy: Jack Oakhurst!

Fortuna: Yes, aunty, and Boston, too. *Catching sight of Skaggs and Stumpy craning their necks over the piano.* What are you hiding there for? *Drags them forward.* Oh aunty, weren't you pleased to see them? Papa Stumpy, wasn't she almost beside herself with joy? *Stumpy half bashfully comes forward. Mrs. Stumpy after a little start, and a gesture of impatience surveys him calmly through her eyeglass. Stumpy offering an embrace.* My dear.

Mrs. Stumpy ignoring the offer: William Henry—ta-ta. Hope I see you, well, pretty tôt tôt.[53] So this is Mr. Skaggs? Been long in Paris, eh?

Skaggs: No, Madame, no.

Stumpy: Well, that beats me—ten years have changed you, Frances Jane.

Mrs. Stumpy: Sorry I can't return the compliment. But don't Frances Jane me. It's mauvais ton.[54]

Stumpy: Have you nothing to say to me, Fran . . . *stops.*

Mrs. Stumpy surveying him: Yes. Go and dress. *Moves to other ladies who have not listened to the above.* Ladies, let us move to the music room. I have given orders that all my *at homes-es* should be shown right into the concert room. I've secured first-rate singers and artistes. Baron—come—you and I will lead the way. Fortuna, help me do the honours. *Exits with Baron.*

Stumpy savagely: I'm sorter tired of this. I'll show them who is the master here. *Offers his arm to the three ladies in turn who without rudeness avoid taking it. Marquise, Madame Pomercy, and Antoinette follow Mrs. Stumpy. Skaggs securely and triumphantly offers his arm to Madame Joubard, who lags behind.*

Skaggs: If you're fond of music I'll take ye to a front pew. *Madame Joubard, about gladly to take his arm, catches Marquise's eye, who turns round and drops him a frigid curtsy. Fortuna, who has gone up to Paul, tries to engage him in conversation.*

Fortuna: You don't want to go in there! Let's stop here. Come and make friends with my two old Fathers. I'll introduce you.

Paul ceremoniously: Pardon me, Mademoiselle. . . . I have hardly as yet been civil to our hostess. Permit me to follow her. *Exits. Fortuna, Skaggs, and Stumpy stand looking at each other—after a pause.*

Fortuna aside: Could Paul be proud . . . and look down upon them? Impossible. *Goes to them effusively and caressingly.* You don't seem a bit glad to see me. *Sadly.* And I was so glad to come.

Stumpy preoccupied, hardly returning her caress: Oh, you're all right, Luck. *To Skaggs.* Come, Pard, this is no place for you and me. We're only interlopers here. We shouldn't have left the free breath of the pines and the pure gold of our valleys for these sickening perfumes and shiny gildings. Come.

Fortuna taking his hand: Don't be a goose. You should have written to say you were coming. No woman likes to be taken unawares. I'll answer for aunty with my life. You know, you can't expect to drop a wife for ten years and then pick her up as you left her.

Skaggs: [line omitted from manuscript]

Fortuna: Here's a telegram in its envelope—look. Perhaps yours.

Stumpy opening telegram: She couldn't even spare time from these new-fangled friends to read a dispatch from her husband.

Fortuna: How did she know it was from her husband? You stupid. Come, dear, don't be so mulish.

Stumpy: It's all the work of that cussed Boston and Oakhurst. Let me just catch 'em!

Servant announcing: Monsieur Colonel Oakhurst.

Stumpy starting: Jack! *Is about to rush joyfully to Oakhurst, stops suddenly, assumes dignified attitude, rejoins Skaggs who draws himself hurriedly up. Oakhurst comes towards them cordially, but seeing their reserve smiles and turns to Fortuna.*

Oakhurst: I have good news for you, my child. I've seen the Judge of Instruction, and Kentuck is a free man. In fact, if it had not been for his own folly in avoiding the Police and an interrogatory which would have cleared him, he need not have been a fugitive. His papers will be returned to him, except one, which implicates another, and he will be here this very night.

Fortuna excitedly: Oh, Jack! Thank you! This is like your dear old self.

Oakhurst aside: May we always keep from her how near and dear once were the two most guilty offenders.

Fortuna glancing at Skaggs and Stumpy: But do you hear? You have not thanked Jack! Jack who has saved Kentuck. Why? They seem ready to eat each other up.

Oakhurst to Fortuna: I wanted to speak with you, my child, but as you are engaged at present, I will retire—later on.

Stumpy furious: Retire! Retire! *You* retire! Look, yer! This is my house—*my* house, paid for with my own money, and if any man's got a right to retire from it—it's Me!

Skaggs furious: Yes, Sir! It's *he! They both go to door. Fortuna interposes.*

Fortuna: Imbeciles. Listen to me. You have no right to leave your house while I'm your guest, and you, Jack, cannot avoid the roof that shelters me. For shame. Is that the Brotherhood of Roaring Camp?

Stumpy: Ask Jack Oakhurst there, if it's like the Brotherhood of Roaring Camp to refuse assistance to a pardner who was poor and in distress.

Oakhurst incredulously: I! I refuse assistance?

Skaggs: Yes. *You*. When you were told at Monte Carlo that Sydney Duck and Dungaree Jack had been followed by a French Police spy, what did you do? Did you challenge the Minister of Police and blow a hole through him at twenty paces, like a man? Eh?

Fortuna indignantly: And do you call it the square thing for a dead shot like Jack to challenge a helpless foreigner?

Skaggs ignoring her: What did he do? Why, insulted them both by offering them money to get out of the country. Brotherhood indeed. *Oakhurst and Fortuna exchange glances. Business.*

Stumpy: And there's Boston. Excuse me! Mr. Adams. Didn't he, me, and Skaggs offer his bank the entire continental agency of the Flying Wild Cat gold and silver Mining Company, and didn't he answer the Bank wouldn't speculate in stocks—and then insulted us by proposing to advance money from his own pocket, if we were hard up. Brotherhood? And when I asked him this morning civilly and like an old Pard if he'd step out and take a cocktail with me at the American bar, didn't he say, people didn't drink spirits in the morning in Paris. *Mimicking Boston.* And wanted me to take a demi-john[55] instead.

Fortuna correcting: À Déjeuner! Oh, Papa Stumpy.

Stumpy: À Déjeuner,[56] or some other drink in the back parlour.

Oakhurst: So as to keep you sober for your first visit to Fortuna.

Skaggs aside: That's so.

Fortuna: Oh, not a word more. You, Stumpy, shall have your cocktail if I have to mix it for you as I used to do in the good old times. If Boston won't let his Bank take stock in the Flying Wild Cat, he shall buy 5,000 shares for me, and Oakhurst shall challenge the first man that dares to criticise me. Come! *Approaches Stumpy who forgetting himself takes her hand, but catching Oakhurst's eye drops it.*

Stumpy turning to Skaggs, with dignity: Let me retire. *Moves towards door. Oakhurst laughing watches them and stops. Fortuna about to detain them.*

Oakhurst aside to Fortuna: Let them go! I promise we'll be fast friends again, before the evening is out. *Skaggs and Stumpy pass him with affected dignity.*

Fortuna: You are going?

Skaggs pompously: To rejoin our friends.

Fortuna innocently: Your friends.

Skaggs: Madame Jobberd!

Stumpy pompously: Monsieur le Baron Trumpy. *Exeunt.*

Oakhurst laughing: Bless their wrong impulsive heads. But they can't help it. Maybe too we are to blame. That prim banker's face of Adams draws on all their old prejudices at sight. But come! How long have they known the Baron?

Fortuna laughing: I'll be bound they never saw their intimate friend before today.

Oakhurst aside: And I shall try that they do not again. *Aloud.* And you? What do you know of him?

Fortuna carelessly: Oh! He is an old friend of Madame Pomercy's and comes constantly to the Villa.

Oakhurst eagerly: An old friend . . . and is he . . . is he in Madame Pomercy's confidence?

Fortuna shaking her finger: Jack! Jack! I believe you are jealous!

Oakhurst: Nonsense! *Aside*. I wonder if the little minx is not nearer the truth than I know. By Jove! I think I am jealous.

Fortuna: Oh, don't alarm yourself! The Baron is claimed elsewhere.

Oakhurst watching her anxiously: Indeed!

Fortuna: Yes. Tony and her mother. They just go for him.

Oakhurst: Ah! Do you know, Forty, I confess frankly, I thought the Baron had not been utterly insensible to the bright eyes of Mademoiselle del Campo Clamoroso.

Fortuna: Why shouldn't you think so?
Oakhurst: Has he ever made love to you?
Fortuna calmly: Frequently.
Oakhurst aside: She expresses too much. *Aloud.* And you?
Fortuna: I . . . oh, I am quite content with the equal love and devotion of my dear guardians.
Oakhurst drily: Ah, that's bad.
Fortuna looking up: Why?
Oakhurst: Because I'm afraid you've given a young fellow reason to think differently.
Fortuna starting: I!! Who?
Oakhurst: Yes. A few hours ago while you were dressing at the Villa Pomercy I was buttonholed by a respectable elderly female on behalf of her son, Monsieur de Lussan.
Fortuna joyfully: Paul!
Oakhurst: I do not think she spoke of him quite as familiarly to a stranger. But then, she was only his mother.
Fortuna eagerly: Yes, yes, and you said?
Oakhurst: Oh, I said, let me see. Yes! I said, you were quite content with the equal love and devotion of your dear guardians.
Fortuna shaking him: Jack Oakhurst!
Oakhurst: Well.
Fortuna: You're a goose!
Oakhurst: But that ain't an answer.
Fortuna: Oh, yes, it is—in Latin. Anser's a goose.[57] Paul taught me that.
Oakhurst: And what else has that admirable scholar taught you? Beside fencing and disrespect of your guardians?
Fortuna: I think, Jack . . . he has taught me to . . . to . . . to like him a little.
Oakhurst: And I daresay he would like to finish your education. *Gravely.* Listen, Fortuna. Paul de Lussan is a young man

brought up in a rigid school of continental propriety—and of course justifies his bringing up by wanting to marry a young girl who defies it. So far, so good. But Paul has aristocratic relations, his mother is one of the old noblesse, while you—

Fortuna embracing him: Have half a dozen of the best, truest parents.

Oakhurst: Unfortunately, a plurality of male parents does not entirely compensate for the entire absence of the female. Has Paul ever asked you about your family? Your mother?

Fortuna quickly: No—no. Why should he? He wants to marry *me*, not a family.

Oakhurst: It is so in America. In Europe, my child, a wedding ring that isn't big enough to go round a genealogical tree is no ring at all.

Fortuna aside: Could *he* be swayed by such notions—no. *Aloud.* Well, Jack, tell him all about me, if you like. But now I must really go to the music room, or Aunty will be furious. *As Oakhurst is about to follow her.* No, don't come in with me, or Aunty will be jealous.

Oakhurst: Some one else might be—to find his privilege usurped. Well, run along. I'll follow you presently. *Exit Fortuna kissing her hand to him.*

Oakhurst alone, looking after her: There she goes and I have not the heart to scold her for her last and greatest folly. I'm getting to be an old fool like the rest, I suppose. *Takes papers from his pocket.* The memorandum of the agency of the Sierra Mine, captured by the Police, and restored to me for Kentuck's benefit. Humph! *Reads.* "500 shares issued to Madame Pomercy 50,000 fr." It might have been more. "5,000 shares to Mademoiselle del Campo Clamoroso, 500,000 fr." Nearly half her capital, and all to swell the pockets of that rascally agent. Upon my word, if we don't get her married soon, and in responsible hands, she'll not only ruin herself, but not leave us enough to give her a position worthy of her. We shall have to take round the hat as we did at Roaring Camp. Well! The call must be met. She must not know that she has been swindled, still less that it was through the connivance of Dungaree Jack and Sydney Duck, her old fathers. But let me once put my hand on the scoundrel of a French agent, and I'll revenge her—if it should be as, I suspect. . . . *Enter Paul. What, the young lover, seeking his divinity*—they are playing at cross purposes. *To Paul.* I can assist you, Monsieur de Lussan. *Paul starts and looks as if he would avoid him. Fortuna has just returned to the concert room.*

Paul embarrassed, coldly: Thank you, Colonel. I have just left it.

Oakhurst smiling: Come, do not be bashful. I am no stern uncle or crusty guardian. I can still understand the feelings of youth *patting him on the shoulder* and sympathise with them. *Silence of Paul frigidly.* Do you not guess that I know all, that I have just seen my ward and *stretching out his hand* that I wish you joy?

Paul not taking the hand with sudden resolution, seeing Oakhurst's surprise: Colonel Oakhurst, I would at any cost have avoided this explanation. It was my intention, & knowing it to be inevitable, to delay it till a fitter moment—but I cannot let you talk to me as you have done. Forget what my mother told you of my intentions, of my hopes—think of me from this hour only as a stranger.

Oakhurst: Monsieur de Lussan. I fail to comprehend. Explain.

Paul with effort: As a man of honour my duty compels me to say that I formally renounce any claims on the hand of Mademoiselle del Campo.

Oakhurst sternly: Sir!

Paul: Permit me to remain silent as to my motives.

Oakhurst: You forget, Sir, that silence is an insult to her.

Paul: Not when I assure you that none is meant.

Oakhurst: And if I insist on knowing what reasons a gentleman can have for trifling with the affection of a young girl?

Paul bitterly aside: Her affection! *Aloud.* Mademoiselle del Campo herself will probably tell you how gladly she renounces a connection which she now feels to be uncongenial.

Oakhurst aside: Is it family pride? The sight of Skaggs, of Stumpy? *Aloud proudly:* Pray, leave the name of my adopted daughter out of this discussion. Neither she, nor I, will, rest assured, have any wish to bind you to *your word*, but once more, will you tell me on what grounds you break off?

Paul: Once more, I will not.

Oakhurst: Then I conclude you are ready to accept the consequences of that refusal.

Paul: I am.

Oakhurst: Enough. You shall answer for it at my time, and my convenience.

Paul: Till then, I shall leave this house—and not again meet Mademoiselle del Campo.

Oakhurst: This is precisely what you must not do. It is not, I presume, your intention to publicly compromise my ward by any sudden change in your manner and attitude before the world. *Contemptuously.* Remain here. *I shall know how to guard her, watch over her, and protect her against the vagaries of a madman or a . . . furious gesture of Paul, immediately repressed at sight of Baron entering—they bow to each other ceremoniously. Exit Paul.*

Baron looking after Paul: I hope I am not driving him away. By Jove, I couldn't stand any more of the screeching in there—apropos, my dear Colonel, allow me to congratulate you. As an American and a republican you may be proud of your victory over our time-honoured prejudices. Upon my word I'd have laid one hundred napoleons[58] to ten that nothing would have brought the Villa Pomercy to Mrs. Smith's salons. Only a word from you to the proud widow, and here we are. For myself, I am an old habitué and quite at home. *Stretches himself full length on a sofa and produces cigar case.*

Oakhurst *drily*: So it seems.

Baron: Have one? *Offering cigars.*

Oakhurst: Thanks. *I* am not at home enough for that.

Baron *aside*: Does our gambling friend intend to give me a lesson? Bah. I can't afford to quarrel with him—just now. *Aloud.* You are modest, Colonel, too modest. Do you affect to ignore the violent impression you have made on the romantic imagination of Madame Pomercy? *She* treats you quite . . . *en ami.*[59] She defers to you, consults you, sees with your eyes. These flattering distinctions tell their own tale. *Foppishly.* I was once honoured with them.

Oakhurst *aside*: Curse his insolence. *Aloud coldly.* If Madame Pomercy has taken me into her confidence, Baron, it is because she has been made the victim of a swindling company known as the Sierra Mine, whose shares have been floated on the European market by a . . . an unscrupulous agent.

Baron *aside starting*: The Devil! How does he know?

Oakhurst *watching him*: Knowing that I had some experience and that I have made it my business to examine the affairs of the company, Madame Pomercy has asked my assistance.

Baron *affecting unconcern*: And you hastened to give it. May I enquire with what success?

Oakhurst still observing him: Not much, I confess. The . . . unscrupulous agent is said to be a man of good social position, which he has used to win the confidence of his victims. I have ample proofs of his connection with the swindlers. I only want to identify him. . . .

Baron uneasily: And then?

Oakhurst: I will give him the option between disgrace and the restitution of his ill-gotten gains.

Baron aside: Hang the man. *Aloud airily.* A most sensational episode on my word—if substantiated. The pretty widow, who has no doubt exaggerated like all women, will I trust not be ungrateful for your chivalrous campaign.

Oakhurst: I act not on her behalf alone. There is in this case a stronger claim yet, the claim of duty.

Baron: Duty!

Oakhurst: Yes—duty. *Confidentially—watching him.* There is one other victim of their fraud for whom I am responsible. I have only quite lately learned that the person I allude to has put every dollar of her fortune into the bottomless pit of the Sierra Mine.

Baron: Her fortune? Whose fortune?

Oakhurst: My ward's. Mademoiselle del Campo.

Baron aghast: Impossible.

Oakhurst: A fact. Deceived by lying reports, the rash, impulsive girl has, without consulting her guardians, invested her all.

Baron aside: That chance gone. *Half aloud.* Nearly duped.

Oakhurst: Oh, entirely so.

Baron: What, Sir?

Oakhurst: Yes. The poor child was entirely duped. What could you expect—a mere girl. *Aside.* I was right. I've got him with both barrels. *Aloud.* But I am boring you with private details that can have no interest for you. I'll leave you to finish your cigar, while I join the Victims. Adams may have brought me fresh information. Baron—not a word of this to anyone. *Moves to Left*. The scoundrel might, if alarmed, take flight and leave the country to avoid the disgrace that will overtake him, his family, and his friends—*Aside at door*. I give him that one chance. *Exits*.

Baron alone: If I ever doubted the interposition of divine Providence, I believe in it now. In another day, I might have been the accepted suitor of a penniless, nameless adventuress surrounded by Brass and spodumene.[60] Fortuna is nothing better. Unable to slide over the disaster of that accursed Mine with my wife's dowry, I should have fallen defenceless into the hands of that Quixotic detective, Colonel John Oakhurst, gambler! *Throws away his cigars*. What's to be done? Take the hint he gives me and run? No! No! That too would be ruin. I have weathered worse storms. I have some trumps left. Thanks to the indiscretion of that old idiot Mrs. Smith, I happen to know exactly who that ward of Oakhurst's is. He might think twice before compelling me to name her mother. Besides, if the game is up with Fortuna, little Joubard is ready to jump down my throat—and her dot, if small, is safe. I might persuade her to elope before the story gets abroad. She is silly. Love making *à la melodrama* would do it. *Stretches himself lazily—then sits down yawning.*

Antoinette entering on tip toe—gazes at Baron. Aside: How handsome and melancholy he looks. *coming forward carelessly*. Fortuna is not here. *Pretending to see Baron*. Oh, Monsieur de Trempes!

Baron aside: This is my opportunity. *Rising with exaggerated emotion. Aloud*. Ah, Mademoiselle, an angel of mercy has guided your steps. Could you have divined how I yearned for one blissful moment alone with you?

Antoinette surprised: With me? No. I did not think you wanted to be ... with *me*.

Baron enthusiastically: Oh yes. I yearned to cast off the mark — to tell you, call you on to me — how I cannot exist without you, whom I adore.

Antoinette aside: How eloquent he is. *Aloud demurely.* Monsieur. Speak to Mamma!

Baron: Cruel child. My passionate love cannot stoop to such cold formalities. None can step between you and me. From your angel lips alone must I hear that you will be my wife.

Antoinette aside: Oh, this is surely the nice American fashion of love making Fortuna told me of. *Aloud.* Oh, Monsieur! What will Mamma say?

Baron: Do not ask her. Be mine forever. You are free, independent. *In a business tone.* Your father's fortune is yours to dispose of, isn't it?

Antoinette: Oh, yes! It was in dear Papa's will.

Baron aside: I thought so. *Enthusiastically aloud.* Let us defy custom. Let us fly, be married mysteriously, at midnight, by moonlight, with torches and depart together unseen to the blue shores of some Italian sea. *Aside.* Auf! That's good!

Antoinette aside: Ecstatic! *Aloud regretfully.* Then — no ball — no ceremony — no bridesmaids — no trousseau.

Baron aside: Little goose. *Aloud.* No! Boundless love, my angel, my queen!

Antoinette aside: How fiery — how irresistible! I did not think he had it in him. *Aloud.* What you propose is an elopement?

Baron: It is, adored Antoinette. A word of opposition from your cruel mother would kill me.

Antoinette aside: This is Elysium! *Aloud innocently.* But Monsieur, Mamma would only be too glad. She has been wanting you to marry me all along.

Baron coldly: Has she? *Aside.* The manoeuvering old shark. *Aloud after a pause.* Ah, Antoinette, if you loved me, you would fall on my breast and sigh, "Adolphe, your wish is my law. I swear that tomorrow I shall be yours."
Antoinette after a short hesitation leans up gracefully against him coquettishly without looking up: Monsieur Adolphe, tomorrow I shall be your wife. *Aside.* The trousseau and parties must come afterwards.
Baron: Angel. *Over her head aside.* Oakhurst and the Mine must stand over for twenty-four hours. *Aloud.* Angel.
Antoinette aside: I like being an angel. *Aloud.* I shall be married in a point lace[61] veil and orange flowers—say, Adolphe.
Baron distant: Oh yes, certainly—they suit this dress.
Antoinette starting up: Pink! Married in pink! Absurd!
Baron taking her back in his arms: Are you not always charming in my eyes? Remember your promise. Tomorrow. Every minute is a century till then.
Antoinette coquettishly: Is this really so? *Aside.* I hope he won't change his mind. *Disengages herself and stretches out both her hands to Baron—he shakes one—she makes him sign to kneel—he reluctantly complies and kisses her hands. Madame Pomercy entering & sees the group—laughs. Antoinette screams, Baron who has not seen Madame Pomercy wonders—Antoinette recovering herself passes Madame Pomercy with demure curtsy—at wing.* Fortuna must know that I have had a real love scene all my own. *Exits.*
Madame Pomercy, coming forward shakes her finger: Incorrigible! I am blind, Baron, and shall be dumb, but it must be the last of your bachelor follies.
Baron rising curtly: A folly in which I am justified.
Madame Pomercy: Yes—so far as encouragement is a justification—but seriously. Listen to me. My mission is fulfilled.

Baron: What mission? Of breaking the hearts of the whole American colony?

Madame Pomercy: Nonsense! Of Ambassadress from the most noble the Baron de Trempes for the hand of Señorita del Campo Clamoroso.

Baron aghast: Good Heavens! Madame.

Madame Pomercy: Calm these transports. You are a successful candidate. The heiress is yours.

Baron: But Madame, this haste, this rashness.

Madame Pomercy: Carried the day. I attacked on all sides. Madame Smith is reconciled to losing you as an admirer, and gaining you as a ward-in-law—she is now securing the vote of her husband (one of those eccentric foreigners turns out to be Mr. Smith) and of his remarkable friend, both being some sort of co-guardians.

Baron interrupting: Those people are of no account.

Madame Pomercy: So I should say. I therefore secured Adams' consent, and can, I think, guarantee the Colonel's. The banker enquired if you cared for pedigree. I said, "Not at all." "For wealth?" I foreswore myself and answered, "Not in the least." Everything is settled so far. Thank me, and run to Fortuna an accepted suitor.

Baron: Nothing is settled! This is absurd, impossible!

Madame Pomercy: Am I dreaming? This language to me?

Baron losing all restraint: I am free—I have not committed myself—

Madame Pomercy: I have—in your name. That is conclusive.

Baron angrily: Even those backwoods savages cannot bind me to this ridiculous connection.

Madame Pomercy: Those backwoods savages might insist upon knowing why you hesitate.

Baron: They might not care to know my reasons.

Enter Marquise and Paul—Baron attempts to withdraw. Madame Pomercy indignantly: No, you cannot go thus. Let my Aunt and my cousin learn on what grounds a gentleman dares to refuse the hand of a girl he had sued for two hours before.

Paul starting forward to Baron: You have not revealed what we saw. *Sign of denial of Baron. To Madame Pomercy sadly.* Adèle, a man may have grave solemn reasons. . . .

Marquise aside: Are we nearing the light?

Madame Pomercy: No, Paul. De Trempes can have none for refusing to marry Fortuna.

Paul: De Trempes! You! You have proposed to her?

Madame Pomercy: Through me! And now he insults us both by a cowardly retraction.

Paul hesitatingly: What . . . pretext . . . has he given?

Baron: None as yet. Must I speak? *Searchingly.* Would you?

Madame Pomercy: If Paul had pledged his word he would redeem it. *He* is a gentleman.

Baron sneeringly: Would he? *Suppressed movement of Paul.*

Marquise coming forward: If my son loved a girl disinterestedly, unselfishly, no consideration of *fortune, parentage,* or *birth* would make him give her up—nothing save her own desire, or the care of her happiness.

Paul wringing Marquise's hand: Thank you, Mother!

Baron roughly: I do not object to any man's pleasing himself by marrying a Californian adventuress—I will not—

Paul hotly: Any man might be proud of winning the love of Mademoiselle del Campo, my mother's friend, my cousin's guest.

Baron brutally: Marry her then—with her low vulgar associates, her obscure birth, her nameless mother—and the manners she has learnt—or inherited.

Paul furious restrained by his mother: Silence!

Madame Pomercy to Baron: Not another such word in my presence! *Aside.* Oh, if Oakhurst were here to put a stop to this.

Marquise quietly: Let him talk on. Let him have his little say. *Half aside.* Amidst the toads and serpents that drop from his lips the pearl of truth may fall. *Aloud.* It is absolutely necessary, especially in this house, to avoid an open scandal, which would compromise us all, the innocent and the guilty—but there is an affectation of mystery which is more compromising still. Monsieur de Trempes, you have said too much or too little. Away with dark hints and black insinuations. Before us, *her friends*, painful as the subject may be, tell us without hesitation what the poor motherless girl has done, or is accused of doing, so that we may stand up and defend her.

Baron to Paul: You hear? Shall I speak? *Paul acquiesces by a sign.* Well, then, and bear me witness you have compelled me to say it, Mademoiselle del Campo has received in her room, tonight, clandestinely, a man who is her lover, and in whose embrace she lay.

Marquise to Paul aside: You knew it?

Paul sadly: I saw it.

Marquise startled: Ah! *After a pause coolly.* And if you did? What then? *Grasps his hand.*

Madame Pomercy: Under my roof—tonight—Dear aunt, what can be done?

Marquise: Nothing at present. *Seeing Mrs. Smith, Stumpy, and Skaggs enter.* Nothing save prevent an outbreak from those people. Baron, be prudent. *Retires left with Madame Pomercy.* Paul, do not stay here. *Exit Paul. They talk anxiously.*

Mrs. Stumpy reacting noisily to Baron, who stands sulkily aloof at right front: Dear Baron! Let me be the first to congratulate you. Fortuna Baroness! My dream realized! I always felt I was born to a title in the family.

Baron evasively: Dear Mrs. Smith—I assure you . . .

Mrs. Stumpy: Of course, I understand it all. My home will be yours. Look upon me as a Mo . . . as an elder sister, and upon William Henry as a Father. *Goes to Marquise and Madame Pomercy and appears to claim their congratulations.*

Stumpy slapping Baron on the back: There's luck to you, old man. And that's to Fortuna. Darn my skin, when the old woman told me you had been hanging round the ranch here, and skirmishing round St. Germain yonder, and been sweet on Forty all this time, I just up and sez, I knew him, sez I, he's one of the real noblesse oblige, sez I, and if Forty and he want to match together, and run in double harness,[62] sez I, I'll give my consent, didn't I, Skaggs?

Baron aside: Curse them. How can I stop this confounded jabber?

Skaggs: You did. But don't you see, you blazing old ruin, that you're only confusing him by your devastating tongue? It ain't the Baronial way to arrange such things first-hand and before all the camp. Your grandmother has got to see his grandmother first, and get a private view of the property. *To Baron.* Don't mind him, Baron Trumpy. But he's not up to the rules of yer demmy monde.[63]

Baron aside: Blockhead! *Aloud.* This gentleman is right. This is not the place, the time, to discuss private affairs. *Expostulate with them.*

Mrs. Stumpy to Madame Pomercy: We shall be, so to speak, connections. I shan't be jealous of your having Fortuna, as we owe you this marriage.

Madame Pomercy coldly: You are too kind. My share in this affair is nothing. *To Marquise.* Dear Aunt, it is getting late. Business.

Skaggs to Baron: That's just what I say. Send along one of your friends to us, and we'll arrange the marriage settlements.

Baron: Marriage settlements!

Stumpy: Of course. You don't suppose that Skaggs and me are goin' to let that gal marry on just what she's got of her own and what Adams and Oakhurst choose to give her? No, Sir! The day she marries, there's a little draft for 50,000 dollars that I hand her over, and an undivided fifth of the Universal Hotel at Frisco.

Baron aside: Ready money! Why did I not let well enough alone. Infernal blunder. *Aloud.* Enough, not now—thanks, but . . .

Skaggs: And I reckon I can see Stumpy's 50,000 and make it 20,000 better. There's nothing mean about me, Pard. Why, you don't reckon we'll let that child of ours marry on a pittance? Besides, you know she's been kinder foolish and lost some of her own money on one of them d—d swindling stocks introduced here by a scoundrelly Frenchman.

Baron aside: What ill luck. *Aloud.* Tomorrow.

Mrs. Stumpy affectedly: Tomorrow, business—tonight, love's young dream. Mr. Smith, I'm ashamed of you, keeping the dear Baron away from his divinity at such a moment. *To Baron.* Let me take you to my sweet child. *Shaking her fan at him.* You wicked, naughty wretch! *Skaggs and Stumpy leading the Baron follow her to door—she turns to Baron suddenly.* Let her old friends prepare her—stop here till we summon you. Ta-ta! *Exits with Skaggs and Stumpy laughing.*

Baron aside: I can manage to escape unperceived and put off explanations till tomorrow. *Looks for his hat and is about to slip off when Madame Joubard enters excitedly and rushes almost into his arms.*

Madame Joubard: Antoinette has told me all, Baron. This is the happiest day of my life. Take my pure angel child, and make her happy. Make her happy. Adolphe! *Weeps.*

Baron awkwardly: Dear Madam. *Aside.* Hang the woman.

Madame Joubard to the others: Dear friends, rejoice in my joy. Antoinette Baronness!

Madame Pomercy looking scornfully at Baron: I understand at last. *To Madame Joubard.* If you are pleased.

Marquise aside: Another villainy. Triumph of the Joubard faction. *Madame Joubard hangs fondly round Baron.*

Madame Pomercy to Marquise: This is intolerable, and I can stand it no longer. One man could, I am sure, unravel this vile intrigue, find out the truth, and speak with an authority which no other possesses. I have lingered here so long only to see Colonel Oakhurst.

Oakhurst entering gaily to Madame Pomercy: I heard my name! May I offer you my arm?

Madame Pomercy impressively: Colonel Oakhurst, I appeal to you to defend your ward, to defend me, her hostess, from the insinuations of that man—*pointing to Baron.*

Oakhurst eyeing him coldly: Insinuations? Madame.

Madame Pomercy: Calumnies. He charges Fortuna with receiving this evening in my house a clandestine visit from a lover and making this a pretext for refusing her hand.

Madame Joubard angrily: As if he had ever dreamt of asking it. Poor Adolphe!

Oakhurst with forced calmness: Who makes this charge against Fortuna, do you say?

Madame Pomercy: Baron de Trempes. *Baron bows defiantly. Paul has returned and leans with folded arms against the arch.*

Oakhurst: I am relieved, Madame. I was indiscreet enough a moment ago to inform him, casually, that you had lost some money and my ward her entire fortune in a swindling speculation. I feared he had betrayed my confidence. I have done him wrong.

Paul aside: Ruined! Fortuna ruined. *To Marquise.* Good Heavens! Could he suspect me of such meanness? *Marquise greets him with a gesture.*

Madame Joubard: Ruined! So even the fortune of the Screeching Field is a sham!

Madame Pomercy to Oakhurst: But the accusation! You are not indignant? You let it pass?

Oakhurst: A little patience, Madame. Monsieur de Trempes could not make an accusation he would be unable to prove. *To Baron.* You are positive? You have a witness?

Baron: I have—two. I have myself, much to my regret—and Monsieur de Lussan.

Oakhurst aside: He! *This* then was his secret. *Aloud.* When did this *clandestine* interview take place?

Baron doggedly: This evening between seven and eight.

Oakhurst: At that hour one of Fortuna's guardians visited her. As he was unfortunately at variance with Adams and myself, whom he knew to be at the Villa, he foolishly effected an entrance by climbing the balcony.

Marquise to Paul aside: You hear! Imbecile.

Paul: Is this true? Or a device to save her?

Madame Joubard ironically to Baron: Pouh! Pouh! Does he think to deceive us with this childish subterfuge? *Aloud.* And no doubt you can produce this new estimable guardian? The fifth? The sixth? Which is it?

Madame Pomercy low to Oakhurst: None but proofs will convince them and clear Fortuna. It is true? Is it not? I feel it.

Oakhurst pressing her hand: Patience! *Aloud.* Madame Joubard is right. I expect this guardian momentarily. Your friend Monsieur de Trempes will identify him.

Baron starting aside: No! Not if I can help it. *Aloud carelessly.* Doubtless a young man in a cloak—embracing Mademoiselle del Campo.

Oakhurst: When you were listening—I beg your pardon—when you watched this interview, how far were you from the window?

Baron: As far as that corridor.

Oakhurst: And it was dark? As dark as this? *Lowers lamps.*

Mrs. Stumpy entering: What is the meaning of this?

Madame Joubard: American juggling.

Marquise putting up her hand warningly: Hush.

Oakhurst having darkened the room: Pardon me, ladies and gentlemen, but as the new guardian is just entering the corridor, I can show you a singular optical illusion. *Appear in the arch Kentuck with hat and cloak walking with his arm round Fortuna's waist. They do not know they are seen.* To Baron. Is that the man?

Baron recoiling aside: The American mining expert. I am lost. *Aloud.* I . . . I . . .

Oakhurst: Do you recognise him? *Aside with suppressed rage.* Or do you want him to recognise you? Speak out—you will have time yet to leave the house and Paris. *Aloud.* Baron, is this the man?

Baron aloud: Yes—it is the same man!

Oakhurst aside: Go—undiscovered. *While all are looking surprised at the two figures in the lightened arch Oakhurst turns up the lamps. After a minute's hesitation Baron makes a gesture of despair and makes his escape unnoticed.*

Paul to Oakhurst imploringly: Who is that man? *Oakhurst puts his fingers to his lips.*

Fortuna advancing holding Kentuck's hand: Come in, darling. They are all friends. I told you so, my dear old Father. *Kisses him and pushes him gently towards Oakhurst and Adams, who has followed her in. They shake him by the hand cordially.*

Paul to Fortuna: Your father! He your father! Oh, how I have been deceived.

Fortuna: Deceived in Kentuck? The kindest of them all. Look at him, the dear old simpleton.

Paul: I thought you had bestowed the priceless gift of your love on one you could not openly acknowledge.

Fortuna: You thought that? You? Paul?

Paul: Oh, forgive me, forgive me—you cannot know how deeply my love, my pride in you were wounded.

Fortuna with energy: Forgive you? Never! Talk of your pride, if you will, but not of your love. What have you seen in me to mean that you dared to suppose I would not openly show my affection for any of the men who stood round my forsaken cradle—who took me to their honest hearts when I was motherless, shared with me their hard-earned bread when there were none to give me food, and later on gave me of their own accord their honourably gotten wealth? Did you think I was ashamed of the homeliest of them all, and that I am not proud of being their child, ah yes, far more proud than you can ever be of your birth, your titles, and your rank?

Madame Joubard: Odious impertinence.

Marquise: Brave child.

Paul: It was not that—Fortuna—not that—I thought . . .

Fortuna: You had no business to think. But look here—let me speak out at last. I am neither so blind or so careless as I seem. I have seen through you all. You barely tolerate those who are kind. *Turning to Marquise* Make excuses for me—others who are not *turning to Madame Joubard* sneer and find fault. Even you, Boston, have lived among them long enough to be doubtful of me—and frightened. It was hard to bear, after you had loved me so long just as I was, in the dear old home, to see you grow estranged because *I* had not altered and couldn't be stiff and fine and fashionable. Oh! Do not deny it! Even at school the girls were supercilious and smiled unpleasantly when they asked me my mother's name. *Her voice breaks.*

Madame Joubard spitefully: A most natural enquiry.

Marquise kindly: And what did you say, my child?

Oakhurst placing his hand on her head: She might have answered truthfully and fearlessly that her mother's name is known all over the hillside of Calaveras as the Benefactress of Roaring Camp.

Fortuna lifting her head proudly: Thank you, Jack. But that is not it. Listen, Madame de Lussan and all of you. My real mother has been Kentuck here, who nursed me on his knee when I was a baby, that great rough man who is gentle as a woman; Stumpy, who gave up swearing and rocked my cradle; Skaggs, who left off drinking and saved his money to buy me finery; Sydney Duck and Dungaree Jack, who if they seem to have forgotten me, and I don't think they have, were loving and loyal then; Dublin Bay, with his rich laugh and Irish songs; French Pete, God bless him, who taught me what I know of his mother tongue; all these, quite as much as Mr. Adams the banker, and Colonel Oakhurst, the diplomat who . . . *facing them defiantly, then suddenly changing her voice.* I love you all the same, Boston and Jack, though you are fine gentlemen.

Adams: My own little Fortuna.

Paul: You misunderstood me, Fortuna. Your friends are my friends, whom I respect and honour—but for one misguided moment, blinded by jealousy, seeing you in the arms of a man whose face I could not discern, I fancied you had another lover, and that my duty was to give you up—

Fortuna explosively: Give *me* up. *Me.* Ah so, you imagine that one hour after listening to words of love from you, I could take another man's kisses. What sort of a creature do you think I am? If this is the way your girls behave it is not mine.

Madame Joubard: Mademoiselle, such a thing would never have been suspected of Antoinette, but when Baron de Trempes himself . . .

Fortuna: And pray who is *he*? What has *he* to say about me? Have I been discussed, hawked about, offered, refused like a beggar . . . an heiress . . . a . . . Where is the Baron—let him face me if he dare. . . .

Adams: He is gone—not to return, my child. Better for all of us. *Looking round—sadly.* I deemed myself more worldly wise than all the others, but I nearly made the same mistake as at Roaring Camp—of wanting to trust you to unworthy hands.

Oakhurst: Hush—all that is past. *Takes Adams off Left.*

Paul to Fortuna: One word of pardon—let me hope. *They move aside, he still pleading.*

Madame Pomercy to Oakhurst: Colonel, you are a wizard. Can you make her relent—

Oakhurst smiling: Love is the greatest magician. *Looking after the two.* You wanted to tame my little girl. Marriage will soon do that.

Madame Joubard to Marquise: You know nothing yet, absolutely nothing of her family.

Marquise: No—not yet—it would be premature—*that* will follow later on.

Kentuck going up to Fortuna: Don't let me spoil sport. Don't you quarrel with your sweetheart, along of me, Forty. Don't do it—it would break my heart.

Paul grasping his hand: Thank you, Sir—thank you—

Fortuna: Ah, Kentuck—*you* would never have suspected me.

Kentuck: No more will *he* again.

Boston: He is a frank and loyal gentleman, Fortuna.

Oakhurst: He loves you, dear.

Marquise coming up to her: Mademoiselle Fortuna, an old woman asks you to forgive her son and to consent to be her daughter.

Fortuna conquered at last extends her hand to Paul, then falls in the Marquise's arms: It seems so strange and sweet to say: Mother!

Madame Pomercy to Oakhurst: Happy child, she loses a fortune, and gains . . .

Oakhurst low: What is offered to you—the lifelong devotion of an honest man.

Madame Pomercy archly: And yet you would not keep the bracelet with "Adèle" at Monte Carlo. *Business.*

Antoinette flying in: Mamma, the Baron is nowhere to be found. What has happened?

Oakhurst to Madame Joubard: Let him be—do not enquire—forget him—take my advice.

Marquise kindly: Antoinette has had a narrow escape—keep your own counsel and remain silent. *Talks with Antoinette.*

Oakhurst attracting the attention of all: Will you all give your consent to Fortuna's marrying Monsieur de Lussan?

Stumpy entering with Skaggs: Who?

Fortuna taking their hands: Why, Paul, you dear old boys.

Stumpy dazed: This one!

Fortuna: This one, of course—stupid.

Stumpy looking round: I say, Forty, there ain't another one anywhere? Eh? It ain't the . . .

Skaggs recovering himself, impressively to Stumpy: Of course it ain't the Baron. Didn't I tell you so all the time? Didn't *he* try to tell you so? It was only their way of speaking for this young fellow. Don't you see—courtin' by proxy like the Royal Families.

Stumpy aside: That's so. Skaggs is right. He did say there was a mistake. Begged me to excuse him. Well, then—*extending hand to Paul* Shake.

Skaggs the same: Excuse him, you know, but he's not up to them yer how tong ways.[64] *Paul, Skaggs, and Stumpy shake hands, then Fortuna joins their hands with Adams and Boston. Business.*

Madame Joubard to Madame Pomercy: I never could endure that de Trempes. Saw through him all the time. *To Mrs. Stumpy.* Fine looking man, Mr. Skaggs. Is he wealthy?

Mrs. Stumpy: Oh, yes . . . a teetotaller.

Madame Joubard to Antoinette: We shall ask him to dinner.

Adams: So, Fortuna, you have the consent and the blessing of all your fathers.

Oakhurst: One moment. Eighteen years ago we gave our Luck her name—today before parting with her to one who will, I trust, guard her life as lovingly as we have done, we can endow her another, which she must bear as nobly as did the man whose dying gift it is—a gift brought to her by Kentuck as a legacy from beyond the grave.

Fortuna: Jack!

Oakhurst producing papers: I have here the last will and testament of our gallant old comrade of Roaring Camp, French Pete. You know how the brave Frenchman died for the cause he espoused in his adopted country—his last act was to bequeath all he possessed to his beloved ward, Fortuna, on the sole condition that she should assume his own family name, and be known henceforth as Fortuna Joubard. Surprise—signed in full—as you can see Pierre Joubard, Colonel, born at Passy, late of Roaring Camp.

Madame Joubard: My scapegrace brother-in-law!

Marquise to Madame Joubard: Your cravings for a family name are satisfied now, I trust, dear Madame.

Madame Joubard: He could not even die like a sensible man.

Madame Pomercy: Welcome among us, Mademoiselle Fortuna Joubard. *Kisses her.*

Fortuna to her Father: But still the Luck—always your Luck, your child.

Kentuck admiringly: The d—d little cuss!

Curtain.

Notes

1. Tailings: debris from milling or mining.
2. Sluice boxes: traps for the sediment from streams of waters in gold mining.
3. "Cast stones at the woman": Jesus says of a woman taken in adultery, "He that is without sin among you, let him cast a stone at her" (John 8:7).
4. Sydney Duck: A slang term referring to an Australian immigrant to the California gold fields who had the reputation for unscrupulous behavior.
5. "Father Mathew temperance medal": Father Theobald Mathew (1790–1856) was a prominent Irish apostle of temperance.
6. Euclid: the father of geometry (ca. 325–265 B.C.).
7. The *Iliad* of Homer: epic poem composed ca. 800 B.C.
8. "Apostrophising": exclaiming words to a person.
9. "Biled shirt": boiled shirt.
10. Siren: a nymph who lures sailors to their deaths; that is, a seductive woman.
11. "Razeed": from French *rasé*. To remove the upper decks of a ship.
12. "Peart": pert or pretty.
13. Antoinette: French Pete suggests naming the child after Marie Antoinette (1755–1793), the queen of France and wife of Louis XVI.
14. Parvenue: upstart.
15. St. Germain: fashionable Parisian neighborhood along the Boulevard St. Germain.
16. *Portières*: doors.
17. *Jardinières*: flower stands.
18. Croesus: a very rich person.

19. Sacré Coeur: Sacred Heart.

20. Tête-à-tête: literally, head-to-head; or a private conversation or meeting.

21. Dot: dowry.

22. "Regilding one's escutcheon": a phrase suggesting a rehabilitation of one's family history or a recovery of one's family fortune.

23. Habitué: a person who frequents a casino, club, bar, restaurant, etc.

24. *Comme il faut*: as it is necessary.

25. *Chevalier d'Industrie*: captain of industry.

26. Alfresco: in the open air.

27. "The firemen made me an honorary member on the spot": Harte alludes here to Eliza (Lillie) Hitchcock-Coit (1843–1929), a popular San Francisco socialite and Paris correspondent of the San Francisco *Daily Evening Bulletin*, who as a teenager became an honorary member of the Knickerbocker Engine Company in San Francisco (*The Exempt Firemen of San Francisco* [San Francisco: Pendleton, 1900], 83–84).

28. Sonata of Beethoven: Ludwig van Beethoven (1770–1827) wrote a total of thirty-two sonatas for solo piano.

29. "2.40 on a shell road": a train speed of two minutes, forty seconds per mile, or a speed of twenty-five miles per hour.

30. "Long Tom rocker": in gold mining, a rocking mechanism in the shape of a trough, some twelve to fifteen feet in length, that replicates panning a stream.

31. "Four aces": four of a kind of the highest card; that is, the highest possible hand in poker, euchre, and other card games.

32. "Beegum": a hollow tree where bees build a hive.

33. "Robinson whiskey": a variety of whiskey distilled by "Jockey Jack" Robinson, in Virginia.

34. "Jimjams": delirium tremens.

35. Yarbs: medicinal plants or herbs.

36. "Give your fist": Shake your hand.

37. "Cold Water Army": a temperance league.

38. Universal Hotel of All Nations in San Francisco: The exclusive Palace Hotel on Montgomery Street in San Francisco opened in October 1875.

39. *Porte cochére*: door of the coach.

40. "Pay gravel": sand with a significant gold content.

41. "Swaller tailed style": formal dress or tuxedo style.

42. Caboodle: lot or collection.

43. Demoiselle: young lady.

44. "They were taking to Europe": they were seeking investors in Europe.

45. "Worth, a fancy dress": Charles Frederick Worth (1825–1895), a French and British fashion designer.

46. Blanc de Perle-Rouge: a pale red ("red pearl") cosmetic.

47. "Noblesse oblige of Paris": the ostensible social obligations of the upper class.

48. *Défilé*: parade.

49. "Painted Jezebel": a woman of loose morals, after Queen Jezebel, the wife of Ahab (II Kings 9:30–37).

50. *Mauvais sujet*: bad subject.

51. *Cafe Chantant*: a music hall or cafe with singing.

52. Longchamp: A Parisian horse racing track or hippodrome, the subject of Edouard Manet's painting "Races at Longchamp" (1867).

53. *Tôt tôt*: very soon.

54. *Marvais ton*: bad taste.

55. "Demi-john": a large bottle of glass or earthenware.

56. *Déjeuner*: lunch.

57. *Anser*: Latin for goose.

58. "Napoleans": Napoleons, French gold coins equivalent to twenty francs each.

59. *En ami*: as a friend.

60. Sponumene: an inexpensive gemstone.

61. Point lace: a form of handmade needlepoint lace.

62. In double harness: a carriage or other conveyance drawn by two animals.

63. "Demmy monde": or demimonde, the class of women who have lost rank because of promiscuity.

64. *How tong*: haut tone or high tone.

PART TWO

The Prince of Timbuctoo

by Sam Davis

Introduction

The Prince of Timbuctoo is a delightful discovery that reveals the literary genius of Samuel Post Davis and attests to the vitality of the Sagebrush School, of which he was an outstanding member. Close to being forgotten for almost a century, Davis's literature is in the process of being revived. As his literature is rediscovered and studied, his life is also being explored. In a word, Davis was remarkable. A versatile Renaissance man, he was a reporter and a fearless and crusading editor; a public-spirited politician and civil servant; a nationally acclaimed historian and syndicated humorist; and a poet, short-story writer, actor, and playwright. In every literary genre that he attempted, he created works that achieve some degree of impressiveness and memorability. Davis's fondness for the theater was never a secret, but until now, no record of what he wrote for it was known. *The Prince of Timbuctoo* is the only one of his dramatic writings to come to light so far, and its quality comes as a happy surprise, like a meteor flashing out of a dark sky. It is a distinguished contribution to a distinguished genre: the American comic opera. As such it participates—worthily—in an older tradition that reaches back from Gilbert and Sullivan to John Gay's *Beggar's Opera*.

Sam Davis was born in Branford, Connecticut, on 4 April 1850, the son of an Episcopal priest.[1] His father, in hopes that Sam would follow him into the church, sent him to a theological school in Racine, Wisconsin, but when Sam was expelled before he could graduate, he was allowed to pursue his interest in journalism. A succession of jobs in Nebraska, Chicago, and, in 1872, California, gave him experience and revealed that in addition to journalistic ability he also had both personal integrity and an audacious sense of humor. Attracted by high wages, Davis soon left California for Virginia City, Nevada, the center of the fabulously rich vein of silver and gold known as the Comstock Lode.

He blossomed in Nevada and immediately found kindred spirits in the journalists who constituted the Sagebrush School, America's long-neglected literary movement. Named after the hardy bushes that subsist in the arid, silver- and gold-rich basin of Nevada, the Sagebrush School began about 1860. It reached its high point in the early 1880s, then declined precipitously in importance thereafter, along with the departure of the transient populations of the mining camps and towns that sprang up wherever there were mines, but lasted only as long as the mineral deposits they exploited were profitable. The Sagebrush School diminished from a flame to a flicker until it was practically extinguished by the death of Davis, its last great practitioner, on 17 March 1918. But the authors who comprised the Sagebrush School in its prime were among the most accomplished in the West. Mark Twain began his literary career in Virginia City and was profoundly influenced in both thought and technique by fellow Sagebrush journalists. Dan De Quille, the most important writer of the Old West after Twain, Ambrose Bierce, and Bret Harte, spent the majority of his life in Virginia City, and was Twain's roommate, mentor, and friend. Joe Goodman, Rollin Mallory Daggett, C. C. Goodwin, Denis McCarthy, and Henry Mighels were other leading Sagebrushers, each distinguished by a flinty morality, personal courage, and wit, as well as by impressive literary ability. Not arriving in Nevada until 1875, Davis was therefore one of the youngest Sagebrushers, but he soon earned the reputation of being one of the most talented.

In 1879 Davis moved to Carson City to help Nellie Verrill Mighels, the widow of the recently deceased Henry Mighels, continue to edit his newspaper, the *Morning Appeal*. Their relationship quickly blossomed into love. Davis married Nellie in 1880, adopted her four children, took over the newspaper, and they subsequently had two more daughters. For the rest of his life, although he was later to travel around the country and to Europe, Davis remained based in Carson City. From there, he wrote prodigiously, and sent out poetry, essays, humorous sketches, and fiction to various newspapers and journals in the West and other parts of the country. At the urging of his friend Ambrose Bierce, Davis gathered together some of his best writing in 1886 and published it as a collection in *Short Stories*, an only partly accurate and overly modest title. It was the only book of his literature that was published in his lifetime. It contains some excellent stories and specimens of humor, but much other good pre-1886 material still remains uncollected, as does everything he wrote afterward, except for his *History of Nevada* (1913).

No bibliography of his work has ever been compiled, and Davis did not keep a record of what and where he published. But he did keep clippings, manuscripts, and some scrapbooks. After he died, his wife piled all his miscellaneous memorabilia into a steamer trunk and stored it away. When she died, the trunk went to their granddaughter, Sylvia Crowell Stoddard. Mrs. Stoddard kept it in her home in Carson City until 1996, when I learned of her in the course of my research on the Sagebrush School, and went to visit that gracious lady on the verge of ninety.

I will never forget my stunned wonder when she led me into the garage, showed me the steamer trunk, and let me open it. I had originally inquired only if she had some letters, photographs, and perhaps mementoes of her grandfather, thinking that perhaps a handful or two might have survived. Instead, the trunk was filled to the brim with literary materials. They were not in any particular order, nor were pages of the same work always clipped together. Overwhelmed at first by the trove, which hereafter is called the Stoddard Collection, I began to sort things out. I worked in her garage for days, separating things into categorical piles: letters, manuscripts, clippings, records, old newspapers, photographs, memorabilia, and so on. Next, I matched pages of manuscripts with one another, and then separated those into genre piles: stories, essays, poems, and plays. Mrs. Stoddard graciously granted me permission to make photocopies of everything and to publish whatever I wanted. It was about a year before I read the typescript of *The Prince of Timbuctoo*. It was poorly typed, and filled with all sorts of insertions, deletions, and mechanical errors, but I saw at once that it was definitely of literary quality. It is my pleasure and privilege now to add it to the record of American literature.

The story of the composition and production of *The Prince of Timbuctoo* is mostly a mystery, and one somewhat complicated by editorial problems. It was far from being Davis's first dramatic venture. Virginia City, Nevada, newspaper archives record an unnamed early play, written before 1879 and obviously intended for local consumption, about a Virginia City newspaper reporter who finds a corpse, hides it to keep a colleague from a rival newspaper from learning about it, and runs into complications with the police. *The Bohemian's Blunder*, another play whose text has not been recovered, enjoyed some local success on the Comstock circuit. *The Sculptor's Daughter* was produced in 1879, but nothing else is known about it. The Stoddard Collection also contains an incomplete but undistinguished manuscript entitled *The Triple Plated Honeymoon: A Chinese Comedy*. Of these and other earlier plays, if there were any, nothing more is known at this time.

The Prince of Timbuctoo, Davis's most ambitious and impressive work for the stage, therefore followed a number of his other dramatic ventures, from which he gained valuable practical experience as a playwright and progressed beyond the beginner and amateur levels. At the time of its writing, there had been at least thirty years of avid theatergoing in the West, the East, and Europe, and Davis had considerable experience as a drama critic and occasional actor. The play was composed in Carson City but not finished until 1905, when he copyrighted a version of it while he was serving as the Nevada State Comptroller and ex-officio state insurance commissioner. Davis's position was not merely a rubber-stamp political appointment, and the record proves it. In 1905 Davis revoked the license of an insurance company from New York for misusing stockholder funds for political purposes, including an attempt to bribe him. He forced the company's president to resign and restore the funds. A year later, when insurance companies tried to pressure California victims to reduce their claims after the disastrous San Francisco earthquake, Davis unilaterally announced that any insurance company that failed to pay one hundred cents on the dollar in San Francisco would immediately lose its license to do business in Nevada. Other states soon followed Davis's lead, and solvent insurance companies decided it was best to honor their contracts.

These actions of Davis's were typical of his entire career; he consistently put the public good first, both as an editor and as an active politician. Inasmuch as Nevada was once so notorious for its open political corruption that it was known as "the rotten borough," an absolutely honest editor and, especially, politician would have had to be a saint. Davis was not a saint but he strove to uphold principle, he did not enrich himself in either politics or journalism, and he was never intimidated by position or power to cover up or gloss over egregious crime. Campaigning, for example, against wrongdoings at the Carson Mint, Davis twice went to jail rather than reveal his sources. And Davis appears to have been the only editor in Nevada to repeatedly attack the wealthy, powerful, and exceptionally dangerous Silver King James Fair for being a murderer, which charge was not substantiated until the Stoddard Collection revealed incriminating evidence from reliable sources.[2] Davis's career therefore is an illuminating backdrop to the political shenanigans of the operetta's villains; the author had firsthand knowledge whereof he wrote.

Like Gay's *Beggar's Opera* (1728), *The Prince of Timbuctoo* takes political and ethical corruption as natural givens and jabs at them off-handedly with swift satiric thrusts. Despite the idyllic picture of Timbuctoo painted by the opening song, it is a kingdom ruled by an arbitrary despot who indulges his whimsical appetites and passions. He is a spendthrift with the public treasury when it comes to pursuing his amours with his gold-digging inamorata Francisera, but he cuts off his only son for falling in love with an honorable woman he does not approve of, and he impulsively sentences people to instant execution for small matters as well as large. Additionally, Markus, a "native shyster lawyer" who will do anything for a price, lives in Timbuctoo. As remote as Timbuctoo is, the real world moves in on it and adds its sophisticated corruption to the relatively naïve endemic kind. In the operetta, England is attempting—not very successfully at this point—to extend its empire over the Boers of South Africa, and its armies need steel bridges over which to retreat. Carnegie Steel, an American corporation alert to opportunities for profit, sends Orndorff and Dooley to Timbuctoo to ascertain which rivers can be bridged and to obtain permission for construction from the local rulers. (The operetta takes liberties with geography in that the British would have had to retreat more than thirty-five hundred miles northwest, far beyond the outer limits of Boer settlement, and far beyond South Africa, for that matter, to reach Timbuctoo and the Niger River.) Dooley has learned the arts of political corruption from the accomplished machine bosses of Boston, Chicago, and Philadelphia, and of the federal government (post office scandals), and is instantly ready to forge wills or buy votes (preferably with fake money but, in a pinch, real money) to serve his employer. Francisera is frankly depicted as an adventuress from San Francisco, an unscrupulous woman who will do anything to gain money and power. Even the virtues of Priscilla Primrose and her six "Puritan maidens" are negotiable: back home they appear prim and proper but in Timbuctoo they confidentially admit that when a little fun's afoot, "One's moral conduct very oft is governed by the latitude."

Satire appears in topical allusions as well. Those about President Theodore Roosevelt tend to be edged. His propensity for hunting game is burlesqued, and the song "Upon the Foreign Beach" at the end of scene 1 of act 3 is sharply critical of American imperialism, by implication the consequence of Roosevelt's "Big Stick" policy. Satiric comments on economic imperialism appear in the references to Carnegie Steel's fishing in troubled international waters. There are satiric jabs at trusts and monopolies, topics of national dispute at the turn of the century, and even an ironic allusion to the extended and scandal-ridden court fight over the will of the silver magnate James Fair, of whom Davis was a courageously outspoken opponent. This court case concluded in 1902, which incidentally establishes that at least part of the operetta's composition took place during or after that year.

Of course the worst that could happen never does because this is a comic opera, and the genial spirit behind it is intent on ensuring that evil schemes go awry, that there can remain a spark of redemptive decency even in would-be villains, and that love triumphs in the end. But this would have been a very different, and lesser, work had the potentially serious matters it touches on been omitted or represented more lightly. Like John Gay, Davis treads a fine line between seriousness and entertainment, subordinates political criticism to comedy, and encourages his audience to laugh at vice and folly while it enjoys the improbable romance of the plot.

The setting of the operetta in Timbuctoo raises the question of possible racism, but literary history, biography, and a reading of the libretto ought to dispel that issue. Timbuctoo was at this time a semi-fabled location, like Zanzibar, Cathay, Araby, or El Dorado, associated with remoteness, exoticism, and riches, and both the quaint-sounding name and the site had some popular appeal. According to Gudde and Bright, as early as the 1850s a prosperous mining town by the name of Timbuctoo flourished in Yuba County, California, the name being inspired either by a local African-American miner nicknamed "Timbuctoo," or by a popular song with the lyric "for he was a man from Timbuctoo."[3] In 1903, the African-American team of Robert Cole and the soon-to-be-eminent writer James Weldon Johnson composed the music and libretto, respectively, for a successful musical, *Whoop dee-doo*, which included the piece "The Maid of Timbuctoo." The song was very popular; it was sung by Lillian Russell at the Broadway Music Hall, and was also adopted by bands into their repertoires. The lyrics of the song do not suggest any connection to Davis's plot other than that the maid was a Zulu, she was "wise" in handling men, and that, of course, she was from Timbuctoo. This last factor, merely putting the name "Timbuctoo" into circulation, is really the best argument for a possible influence on Davis. Interestingly enough, however, it is more possible that *The Prince of Timbuctoo* might have influenced a 1914 musical farce, *The King of Timbuctoo*, by Leon O. Mumford. An untalented work without wit, and otherwise forgettable, *The King of Timbuctoo* does have enough thin similarities in setting, cast, and plot to *The Prince of Timbuctoo* to at least raise the question of influence. Be that as it may, however, added to the other uses of the name, it does establish that Timbuctoo had a basis in popular culture both before and after Davis's comic opera, as well as in the very years in which it was being composed.

If the libretto is examined, it will be seen that the entire operetta uses racial epithets only a very few times, of which only one, devoid of malice, might be traced to the author; the offensive ones are all chargeable to the characters. It is tempting to speculate how this operetta might have been cast and played in Carson City. There is next to no condescension toward Africans and, by implication, African Americans, nor is there any of the demeaning stereotyping of appearance, language, or mannerisms that characterized minstrel shows and representations of blacks in American vaudeville, radio shows, and movies of the early part of the twentieth century. Judging from the casualness with which the interracial amours of the plot develop, the operetta is astonishingly and refreshingly free of racism. The copyrighted version of the text gives the prince a "strawberry mark" above his left knee, a detail that would have been indiscernible had color been a major feature of make-up or used exaggeratedly to imply racial inferiority. In this work, Festicus is simply an idealistic lover who happens to be African. Furthermore, he is better spoken than any of the other characters, some of whom speak a slangy Americanese, and he is especially more articulate than Dooley, whose Irish vernacular is pronounced. Zulu Lou is a pert and attractive young woman, period, and Orndorff as well as Festicus is attracted to her. She is high-spirited and conscious of her wealth and family influence, but her love for Festicus is sincere and never wavers. Whatever Davis's prejudices might have been, anti-black feeling was not one of them. For years, Davis was a close friend of Mary Ellen "Mammy" Pleasant, a distinguished and most influential African-American citizen of turn-of-the-century San Francisco, and an important pioneer of civil rights in California. That Davis also participated in that cause is evidenced by a remarkable and possibly unprecedented apology he made to "all the colored people in America" for an unauthorized and racially insulting article that appeared in his paper while he was away.[4]

If anything, the operetta leans rather heavily on the Irish valet Peter Dooley, a Machiavellian graduate of American ward politics. A bigot who looks down on the natives of Timbuctoo, hates Chinese, and fawns over whomever has power in Timbuctoo, Dooley bears little resemblance, beyond a shared last name, to Finley Peter Dunne's classic creation, Martin Dooley, the ironic bar-owning philosopher of Chicago's Archey Road. The political schemer Dooley continues to plan to do Carnegie's dirty work even at the end, and after his boss Orndorff decides to allow himself to enjoy life in Timbuctoo. (Yet even Dooley has redeeming qualities, which he demonstrates by his resourceful assistance to Orndorff and the cause of the young lovers.) Compared with Martin Dooley's pungently ironic vernacular, Peter Dooley's Irish dialect is weak and inconsistent, and when Zulu Lou impertinently uses the Irish word *forninst* (against) in conversation with Dooley, the joke is on him. In the final analysis *The Prince of Timbuctoo* contains no more negativity toward blacks than *The Mikado* does toward Japanese. Timbuctoo is simply a place far enough off the beaten path to be exotic and susceptible to the free play of Davis's artistic imagination.

There appear to have been some models that Davis followed in composing *The Prince of Timbuctoo* but in the absence of specific information about his library and his reading, these can only be inferred. Like many of the Sagebrush authors, Davis was an autodidact. His scope of reading of classic and familiar literature, particularly of novels and plays, was substantial, probably beyond that of most college graduates of today. Gilbert and Sullivan are almost certainly in the background of *The Prince of Timbuctoo*; it would be astonishing if such an active theatergoer as Davis had not seen some of their productions either in America or England. From the libretto's references to decapitation and, in the copyrighted version of the play, the hero's vaguely Japanese-sounding name of Hammagassiki, it is quite likely that Davis was familiar with *The Mikado* (1885). The eclipse of the moon in act 3 has close parallels, both verbal as well as situational, to Mark Twain's use of the eclipse of the sun in *Connecticut Yankee* (1889), and Davis, as a personal friend of Twain's, might be supposed to have read that novel. Of course, the conventional and frequent use of the moon in literature as a symbol of romance, infatuation, temporary lunacy, and change also might have fed independently into the operetta's last act, but the eclipse is an unusual detail. Finally, the similarities to Gay's *Beggar's Opera* should not be overlooked. If Davis did any checking into the literary history of the comic opera tradition that Gilbert and Sullivan followed—and it would be atypical of him if he did not—he would have encountered Gay's classic work. Beyond its general appeal to him on the basis of its wit and irony, Davis might also have adapted one of its most famous scenes. It occurs in one of *Timbuctoo*'s final duets, "Two Hearts that Beat in One Ragout," in which Festicus and Zulu Lou sing of how sweet it will be to be barbequed together. This is reminiscent of act 3, scene 15 of the *Beggar's Opera*, in which Polly and Lucy sing a tender but equally sappy romantic duet about wishing to be hanged with Macheath.

A lifelong and avid theatergoer and sometime actor, Davis undoubtedly attended many performances of the comic operas that were popular then in America and Europe. Besides the works of Gilbert and Sullivan, and Gay, he was also probably familiar, at the very least, with the immensely popular *Black Crook*, a famous American musical, and the comic operas of John Philip Sousa and Victor Herbert. It would not be necessary for those and similar works to have been performed in the West; Davis could have seen them on his travels to the East Coast and overseas. Musical comedies owed some of their popular appeal to scantily clad actresses, suggestive lyrics, and dances never seen in sedate settings, and that Davis incorporated these features into his play is evidence of the influence of the living genre upon him. But unlike many of the comic operas whose plots were either pure escapist romanticism or fantasy, *The Prince of Timbuctoo* has, as we have seen, an agenda of social and political criticism that gives it more complexity and depth. Its libretto, therefore, is its forte, and although many of its lyrics are perfectly adaptable to music, none of them have been immortalized as songs.

Unfortunately missing from this comic opera is its musical score. Printed on the title page is the note "Music by Rosalind

Richmond and Chas. Kohlman." To date, research has not found any information about either composer, let alone their music. Given the number of songs in the operetta and their strikingly lyrical qualities, this is a most regrettable and frustrating omission. If the original score is not recovered, producing a new one might make a worthwhile challenge for some latter-day composer.

Our text of the work is based on the Stoddard Collection version. A copyrighted version dated 1905 exists, but internal and biographical evidence suggests that the Stoddard text also probably dates to 1905. Working with any manuscript of Davis almost always requires editorial intervention for a variety of reasons, and this text is no exception. The most important one is the typical lack of a fair copy. Davis's handwriting is notoriously bad—very close to illegible. In addition, even with typescripts, his spelling and punctuation are atrocious, and missing or transposed words are not uncommon. Both the Stoddard typescript and the Library of Congress copyrighted version abound in mechanical errors, and deletions and insertions are also frequent in both. Printers in Davis's time often had impressive copyeditor skills, and those who worked with Davis needed them. Indeed, one of the mysteries of Davis's career is who corrected his manuscripts during his more than forty-five years of activity; there had to have been constant editorial assistance from printers or perhaps his wife.

One more reason for editorial intervention with Davis's manuscripts is that he often continued to alter a text even after it was copyrighted or published, and some of those changes resulted in substantial improvements. Such is the case with the fluid text of *The Prince of Timbuctoo*. From the number of changes even in the copyrighted version, it is clear that it is a draft. For the same reasons, the Stoddard version is also a draft but, in my opinion, it is significantly superior to the other, both aesthetically and in content, and as an improvement is probably a reworking of the copyrighted version. The editorial changes I have made in it have been restricted to proofreading corrections of obvious solecisms, insertion of a few omitted words, and the standardization of names and designations of speakers.

If his habit of negligent composition seems inconsistent with regarding Davis as a noteworthy literary figure, it can be explained as one of those occasional paradoxes of literature, in which the writings of worthy authors are buffed into shape by editors who thus rescue literary jewels from solecistic surface blemishes. If Davis's style requires polishing, however, it is plain from the texts that they are worth the editorial help, and that the sparks of undeniable imagination, wit, depth, feeling, and skill, which are present in his works from the beginning, are his alone.

Although information regarding the performance of *The Prince of Timbuctoo* is presently lacking, the fact that it was copyrighted is presumptive evidence that Davis intended it for performance. The existence of two versions might be attributed to the possibility that Davis revised the copyrighted text in preparation for the comic opera's performance, but this is only conjecture. The copyrighted version, for example, lists the hero's name only as Hammagassiki, and his father's name as Zezas, whereas the Stoddard version inconsistently uses two names for both characters. In the unmodified Stoddard text Festicus is the hero's name for most of the play, but Hammagassiki is used briefly in act 2, and the father's name begins as Heggamaggar (a verbal echo of "huggermugger"?) but is switched to Zezas halfway through act 2. (Our text replaces the occasional alternate name with the predominant one.) Clues like these indicate only that Davis was undecided on names, but do not give enough direction for secure conclusions.

What is certain, however, is that *The Prince of Timbuctoo* is a sprightly work of impressive talent as well as being a unique specimen of its genre, and a significant contribution to literary history. Its plot is charming, its characters engaging, its libretto is sophisticated, and its lyrics are delightful and trenchantly witty. The discovery of this sparkling achievement by Sam Davis, one of the most accomplished authors of the Sagebrush School, is further evidence that its literature, after years of being lost or neglected, has innovative and sophisticated authors and works that are belatedly but assuredly enriching our national culture.[5]

NOTES

1. The biographical information for this and following paragraphs comes from my biographical sketch, "Samuel Post Davis," in *Nineteenth-Century American Fiction Writers, Dictionary of Literary Biography*, ed. Kent P. Ljungquist (Detroit: Gale, 1999), 92–99.

2. The editor is presently editing a book manuscript of Comstock memoirs that will present the evidence in its James Fair Appendix.

3. See Erwin C. Gudde, *California Place Names*, 4th ed. rev. and enlarged by William Bright (Berkeley: University of California Press, 2000), 338.

4. "Indignant Colored Men," *Midwinter Appeal*, 17 February 1894, 3:1. This paper was published by Davis as part of the '49 Mining Camp concession of the California Midwinter International Exposition of 1894.

5. Since 1981, I have published a number of articles on, and editions of recovered works by, such Sagebrush authors as Dan De Quille, Joseph Thompson Goodman, Rollin Mallory Daggett, C. C. Goodwin, Alfred Doten, James W. E. Townsend, and, now, Sam Davis. Daggett and Goodman's daringly advanced play, *The Psychoscope*, will be published by the *Mark Twain Journal* in 2006. The project mentioned above in note 2 will be a major addition, when published, to the growing body of recovered Sagebrush literature.

The Prince of Timbuctoo
A Comic Opera in Three Acts
Libretto by Sam P. Davis
Music by Roselind Richmond and Chas. Kohlman*

PLOT

Daniel Orndorff of New York and his valet Peter Dooley arrive in Africa as agents for Carnegie & Co. to explore the beds of rivers to find suitable sites for steel bridges over which the British Army can retreat after losing battles with the Boers.

Arriving in Timbuctoo about the same time as an adventuress who has known the King of Timbuctoo in Paris, a contest begins between Orndorff and his valet, and the adventuress for the political control of the Kingdom.

The adventuress secures the services of a shyster lawyer and the two forge a number of wills in favor of several different persons. These documents purport to be from the King. One will, in which he bequeaths all his wealth and title, throne and scepter to Francisera, the adventuress, is written on asbestos paper. When the adverse wills are submitted to a trial by fire it survives the ordeal. The King having been poisoned in the meantime, she is proclaimed Queen of Timbuctoo.

Orndorff and his valet, fathoming the trick by which she has acquired the throne, arrange a counter plot. Dooley, who has been made Supervisor of Elections before the King's death, calls an election after first persuading the Queen that she will be unable to hold the throne without first having acquired a vote of confidence from the

---

* Musical score has not been found. See pp. 141–42 above.

people of the Kingdom. He betrays her by allowing the ballot box to be stuffed against her, and she is defeated by a heavy majority.

Realizing that she is beaten, the Queen announces that the votes will not be counted until the first of the month, at which time there will be a return to the ancient customs of their forefathers and a barbecue of human flesh will celebrate the event. Thus she expects to appeal to the superstitions of the natives and also dispose of her enemies.

Among these is the son of the King, whom she has deprived of the throne, and a Zulu girl with whom the Prince of Timbuctoo has fallen in love. Prior to his death the King banished the Prince for forming an attachment with the Zulu maid.

The Queen attempts to win the affection of the Prince and fails because of his love for Zulu Lou.

Prior to the counting of the ballots and the celebration of the barbaric feast, the Queen has arrested Orndorff, Dooley, the Prince, and the Zulu maid on the charge of treason, and arranges to serve them up at the feast.

An eclipse of the moon taking place at exactly the same hour enables the condemned people to appeal to Heaven for justice. The eclipse coming on at the right time so works upon the superstition of the natives that they dethrone the bogus Queen. The Prince and his bride ascend the throne as the darkening of the moon passes away, and the drama closes happily.

Cast of Characters

Festicus Prince of Timbuctoo, banished from the Kingdom because of a love affair with a Zulu maid of lowly birth

Heggamaggar King of Timbuctoo, put out of the way because of his station

Francisera an adventuress from San Francisco, who acquires the throne of Timbuctoo by fraud

Zulu Lou a Zulu maiden in love with the Prince

Daniel Orndorff an agent for Carnegie & Co.

Peter Dooley a Chicago politician, and his valet

Markus a native shyster lawyer

Priscilla Primrose of Boston, and her six Puritan maidens

Attendants, dancing girls, members of the Royal household, etc., etc.

Scene: Timbuctoo on the banks of the Niger
Act First. The Conspiracy
Act Second. The Election
Act Third. The Eclipse

Act First

OPENING CHORUS

Scene. Banks of the Niger in the foreground. King's Palace in the background.

Chorus:
If the outside world half but knew,[1]
The wealth we store in Timbuctoo,
The grub we eat, the drinks we brew,
The times we have, the stunts we do,
Then Christian, Turk, Gentile and Jew,
Would come and camp in Timbuctoo.
  In Timbuctoo, In Timbuctoo,
   Buctoo, Buctoo.

Inhabiting the jungles dense,
We run the same at small expense.
We lie all day and take our ease,
Mid monkeys, snakes and chimpanzees,
And feel quite sure you would not rue
A summer spent in Timbuctoo.
  In Timbuctoo, In Timbuctoo,
   Buctoo, Buctoo.

We have no treason in our ranks,
No temperance or suffrage cranks,
Pink teas, receptions, balls and hops,
Lotteries, tan games, bucket-shops,[2]
These roses all your pathway strew,
When once you come to Timbuctoo.
  To Timbuctoo etc.

Life is a round of fond delights,
Horse racing, football, finish-fights.[3]
The land of gold and gems and flowers,
Where pleasure's wand directs the hours.
If you would all your youth renew,
Then come and camp in Timbuctoo.
    In Timbuctoo etc.

Life is a round of sweet content,
We scarcely ever pay our rent,
The town is full of winsome jades,
The woods just swarm with pretty maids,
With these attractions not a few,
You'll find no flies on Timbuctoo.
    On Timbuctoo etc.

Enter Francisera, disguised as a female book agent.

Fran.: I wonder if the King will recognize me in this garb. It's some time since we met in gay Paree. Those were happy days when we made such a gaping hole in the treasury of his kingdom. He showered me with blazing gems, all of which I have been obliged to hock to get here. I hear he is getting old and his throne is toppling. If I could only comfort his declining years he might remember me in his will. [*Enter Markus dressed in black tights, claw hammer,[4] and battered plug hat, law book under his arm.*]

Mark.: [*Approaching Fran from behind.*] Did you speak of wills, Madam?

Fran.: I was mentioning the matter of wills but I was not addressing you.

Mark.: Then my dear girl it's high time you were addressing me. If you want a will that will hold water and stand the legal gaff and be air tight and copper riveted, come to me. If you want a King's will hot off the stove, fixed any way to suit, and done to a golden brown come to the bakery where the dish can be served right. [*Presents his card.*]

Fran.: [*Reading.*] "Mark Markus Attorney-at-law, Timbuctoo. Counselor to the King. Office—attic of the King's palace prior to ten o'clock A.M." And where, pray, after that?

Mark.: You'll find me at the Royal Brewery after that.

Fran.: Am I to infer that you could forge wills?

Mark.: As a manipulator of that branch of the legal profession I stand without a peer.

Fran.: Don't you think it awfully wicked to forge wills?

Mark.: It might be in the highly moral United States, but there seems nothing against it in the Code of Timbuctoo. [*Opens his book.*] And I have studied it from end to end.

Fran.: But have you no compunctions, no principles?

Mark.: Divil a bit, Madam.[5] I'm a lawyer and out for the stuff.

Fran.: [*Rushing forward and embracing him.*] At last I have found the man I have been looking for. Link your fortune with mine and we will rule the empire.

Mark.: Well, make a partnership proposition and get down to business. What's your game?

Fran.: It is a desperate one. I love social standing, adventure and money. I hail from San Francisco and if you can help me, I can run this little kingdom of Timbuctoo. Is it "yes" or "no"? And be quick about it.

Mark.: I'll stay with you to the finish for about fifty percent gross. [*They shake hands.*] Ever meet the King?

Fran.: We spent a winter together in Paris.

Mark.: Ah, ah. That must have been the winter that required a raise in taxation to meet expenses. We all remember that winter. That is, the taxpayers remember it. The winter of nineteen hundred.

Fran.: The same, and I shall never forget it, either.

Mark.: The forged will trick is the thing. I will forge about ten different wills in favor of ten different people. And all supposed to be the King's will, bequeathing everything in sight to various people: crown, throne, scepter, lands, gold, and ivory.

Fran.: Exactly.

Mark.: What will be the state of the King's health for the next few weeks?

Fran.: He's liable to have a sort of tired feeling, I think.

Mark.: And a few dizzy spells. Well, after he croaks from the malaria and such, there will be ten wills come to the fore and we will submit them all to a trial by fire. That's the way out here when there is any dispute. But the will that stands the test will be written on asbestos paper and survive.

Fran.: That will be *my* will.

Mark.: That will be *our* will, my dear woman. We'll have the contract all fixed up. Now get an audience with the old fellow as soon as you can and I'll tend to the rest of the work.

Fran.: You have a great head and I will ever be indebted to you for your assistance in this matter.

Mark.: You will never be indebted to me a minute for I will begin copping my commission as soon as you get yours. You are dealing with no Mendocino County farmer this trip.[6] Here he comes now. I'll duck out. [*Exit Markus. Enter Heggamaggar, King of Timbuctoo.*]

Heg.: [*Starting.*] What, a strange woman in my realm? I must call the guards.

Fran.: Never mind the guards. You did not have any in Paris.

Heg.: As I live, 'tis Francisera, my old flame who wintered with me in Paris.

Fran.: You were a prince then and I felt that we were equals, but you sit upon a throne now and I wondered in my heart if I might not be trespassing upon your royal favor.

Heg.: Did your heart tell you nothing else?

Fran.: Only that I loved you still. [*Advancing with outstretched arms.*] My love, my life. [*They embrace.*]

Heg.: Tell me, adored one, everything that has happened to you since we parted.

Fran.: [*Aside.*] Well, he don't want much, does he? [*To Heg.*] Well, dearest, I have been married and divorced. When I wedded my husband he had a great deal of money but after a while . . .

Heg.: He didn't have as much, eh?

Fran.: How can you . . . ?

Heg.: Well, we won't mind that. Tell me, Fran, can you sing me something new from the United States? I'm dead tired of Dolly Gray, Mary Green, and Hiawatha[7] in Timbuctoo for the last year. Do give me something fresh!

[*Solo. Fran.:*]
<u>Here's to the Good Long Green.</u>[8]

People we meet of all kinds and sorts,
When we travel about the swell resorts,
My hub[9] was the kindest that ever was seen,
For he gave me lots of the good long green.

>*Refrain:*
>>Then here's to the good long green!
>>May our purses never be lean
>>While pleasure can be bought
>>Let us hope we'll ne'er be short—
>>Be short of the good long green.

In Newport surf, July nineteen,
I swam where the breakers were cold and green,
You will see for reasons I soon will state,
I well remember the day and date.

Covered with foam from top to toe,
I soon slid down where the corals grow.
And there to my complete surprise,
Encountered a monster with big glass eyes.

When he put his flipper about my waist,
I felt that the member was not misplaced.
Though really I should have struck for shore,
I held my breath and sighed for more.[10]

To the same place daily I used to scoot,
To meet that man in the diver's suit,
And of all the tourists that sniffed the sea,
Not a single lobster was on to me.

But later I learned to my huge disgust,
Of a diver's club that had formed a trust.
And so 'neath the restless slippery sea,
Some forty men had made love to me.

Heg.: Some day we will have that sung in Court to relieve its awful solemnity. Let us retire and talk things over. [*Places his arm about her.*]

Fran.: But might not my presence in Court give rise to some heartburnings? Might not the heirs object?

Heg.: There are no heirs. My only son, the infernal scapegrace, fell in love with a brazen Zulu girl and he had other bad habits: gambling, drinking, and . . .

Fran.: Trips to Paris?

Heg.: Yes, trips to Paris. The young scamp conducted his dissipation openly and when reproved by me had the effrontery to tell me that he was merely a chip off the old block. He dragged down the royal purple. While I went the pace in Paris I was incog and conducted myself quietly so to speak, er . . . [*Both burst into a fit of laughter.*] Besides . . .

Fran.: You were never found out. Ha, Ha, Ha.

Heg.: Come, let us be going. I would a word or two with thee. [*Exeunt Heg. and Fran. Enter Daniel Orndorff, Dooley, Long Stop and Short Stop. Orndorff dressed in a diver's suit. Orndorff and his valets carry an air pump and hose attached to the diver's suit. Orndorff enters the water and the pump is placed in position.*]

Dooley: This is the first time I was iver chonnected with the divin' indhustry. Whin I heard that me man was to explore the river beds of Africa to build steel bridges for the English to retrate over, I say here is a groin' indhustry for the British are continually gittin' licked in new places, and findin' that Andrew Carnegie[11] was backin' the plan, I hooked up to it at once. Every time the British git licked, up goes the stock of the steel combine. [*Enter Zulu Lou who, not noticing the others, approaches the water's edge and prepares to take a bath.*]

Lou: I wonder if I will have time for a quiet dip in the river while these infernal Court ceremonies are going on? [*Sings.*]

Mother may I go out to swim?
> Yes my darling daughter,
Hang your clothes on a hickory limb,
> But don't go near the water.

When the Court takes a bath here there is no end of the flummery, but when I tackle it I just shed my clothes and take a header. I must hurry and get out before the Prince comes. The old King banished him, eh? Well, he will be here by two o'clock in disguise, so he wrote me. There's over an hour yet. [*Sits down and prepares to remove stockings.*] Wonder if he's watching me. Wouldn't it be awful? Come to think it wouldn't be as bad as if somebody I didn't know was snooping round. [*Orndorff steals up the bank in his diver's suit and places his arm round her waist.*] Oh, my! What's that? It must be Festicus himself. No one else would dare to take such liberties with me as this. [*Draws arm about her.*] He said he would be disguised and this certainly must be him. [*Nestles up to Orndorff.*] It's nice anyhow. [*Dooley at the pump catches sight of the pair and lets go the pump handle in astonishment. As he does so, Orndorff's arm falls away from Zulu Lou. One of his valets grabs the handle and resumes the pumping. At this the arm resumes work on the girl's waist. All the lovemaking is dependent upon the manner in which the handle is worked.*]

[*Duet. Lou and Orn.:*]
Lou: I hung my clothes on a hickory limb
> And stood there all in a shiver,
For I had concluded to have a swim,
> In the cool, inviting river.

Orn.: You feel like saying dammie
      When the water is cold and clammy
          But you'll have a good time
            With the frogs and the slime
  If nobody tells your mammie.

Lou: So I left my embroidered togs
        With all their tucks and frills,
  To have some fun with the pollywogs
        And run the risk of chills.

Orn.: Though we knew each other but slightly,
I came up quite politely,
      Though apologies may be due
      I trust that I don't to you,
Appear as a thing unsightly.

Lou: Festy, I wasn't the least surprised,
      When I felt your arm around me.
I knew in a minute 'twas you disguised,
      And was mighty glad you'd found me.

Orn.: If I'm not too officious
The time is quite auspicious
      And a long drawn kiss
      About like this [*Kisses her.*]
Oh, wasn't that delicious?

[*During the rendition of this song the pump handle is worked in turn by Dooley and his valets, the music rising and sinking with the way the pump is worked. When Orndorff ceases to make love to the girl by reason of the air supply running low, she motions behind with her hand to the operators on the pump to get to work. As the last line is sung, enter Prince Festicus wearing a suit of American clothes of some large checked design.]*

Fest.: What do I see! Zulu Lou receiving attentions from a monster! [*Lou shrieks in terror and falls to her knees.*]

Lou: Oh, Festy! Is this you? There's nothing wrong.

Fest.: Can't I believe my eyes?

Lou: Would you believe your eyes against the word of your own Zulu Lou?

Fest.: Possibly I'd better go to a Sanitarium and take a course of treatment for my eyes. [*Advancing to Orn.*] You seem to be somewhat in evidence here. [*Strikes him.*]

Doo.: Give him a go, Dan. I'll furnish all the air you need. [*Orn. strikes a pugilistic attitude and lunges out while Dooley begins to work the pump while they fight.*]

Lou: Listen. [*Noise of shouting.*] Here they come! Fly while you have time. The King! The King! You will be executed. Fly and when we meet I will explain everything. [*They embrace and Festicus rushes from the stage.*] [*To Orn.*] Fly or your life is not worth a straw.

Orn.: [*Grasping her about the waist.*] We will take to the water together and when the King comes I will be rescuing you. It's our only chance.

Lou: Correct. Get a move on. [*Falls in his arms.*] Hurry or the crowd will be dead on. [*They take to the river together. Enter a crowd of natives with a blare of trumpets and music.*]

Natives: Make way for the King. Make way for the King. [*Enter King followed by crowd of retainers.*]

Doo.: Save her! Save her! Help! Help! There's somebody drowning in the river! [*Orn. emerges from the stream with the limp body of Lou in his arms. People on the stage crowd to the bank and show great excitement.*]

Heg.: It's that infernal little witch that so disturbs my kingdom. Why didn't he let her drown and be done with [her]? What in the deuce is this anyhow, a strange fish?

Orn.: It is a diver's dress for exploring the river beds.

Lou: It was a gallant rescue, your Majesty. I was sinking for the last time and my life seemed to pass before me like a panorama . . .

Heg.: If your life ever gets into panoramic form it will be a dandy attraction on a Midway show.[12] [*To Orn.*] Be at the Palace with your gang as soon as you can get into some Court togs. *Aside.* I've some curiosity to know if that's my son inside that aquatic costume. [*To the natives.*] After I leave here you fellows investigate that mud turtle and see what's in the shell. Have all hands at the Palace front steps as soon as possible. [*Exeunt King and retainers, leaving a few natives. As soon as the King is gone the natives proceed to fish Orn., represented by a dummy, out of the water and after trying to get the diver's suit open, fall upon it with drills and cold chisels and inserting some gun powder, blow it up. The dummy rises in the air out of sight with the explosion and Orn. comes down on the stage clothed in rags and tatters and blackened with gunpowder. As he hits the stage he sings to the people on the stage. The people listen and applaud.*]

[*Solo. Orn.:*]
<u>When We Come to Settle Down in Timbuctoo.</u>

> Although a perfect stranger,
> I think there's little danger
> >   In falling in with people such as you.
> So I'm glad to meet you pard,
> And, old Hottie, here's my card
> >   For I've come to settle down in Timbuctoo.
> > *Chorus:*

He's come to settle down in Timbuctoo.
  In Timbuctoo, In Timbuctoo.
He's come to settle down in Timbuctoo.

A man about my size,
Just tumbled from the skies,
  To which a little while ago you raised me.
I was sent across the sea,
By the firm of Carnegie,
  And so the last explosion didn't faze me.
   Chorus.

The house I travel for
Helped to bring about the war,[13]
  And when the tariff boosts the price of steel,
The fellows of the trust,
Just gather in the dust,[14]
  And make their millions humming off the reel.
   Chorus.

While knocking at your gate,
We will boost your real estate,
  And make a dollar do the work of two.
Votes will be bought and sold
With the chink of shining gold,
  When we come to settle down in Timbuctoo.
   Chorus.

We will raise the price of wool,
For we have the proper pull
  And know just how to put the measure through.
We will lift the price of wages
And you all will ride in stages
  When we come to settle down in Timbuctoo.
  Chorus.
[*Encore verses.*]
We'll dispense with bums and tramps
And have incandescent lamps
  With novelties this happy land we'll strew.
You'll have lots of fun and frolics
And your babies skip the colics
  When we come to settle down in Timbuctoo.
  Chorus.

Every girl will have a beau
And your postage will be low,
  When you come beneath the red and white
  and blue,
And the taxes of this land,
Will be lowered to beat the band,
  When we come to settle down in Timbuctoo.
  Chorus.

Every hut becomes a mansion,
All resulting from expansion,
  And this change of life you'll never, never rue.
We'll forgive you all your sins,
And your wives will all have twins,
  When we come to settle down in Timbuctoo.
  Chorus.

Orn.: I hope these people will excuse us until we have time to get ready for the royal reception. [*Exeunt natives.*]

Doo.: Wasn't that a great explosion? I thought for a while you was goin' to Heaven to stay, but still I was perfectly calm and collected.

Orn.: I thought at one time they would begin to collect me. But where are those court togs you brought from the costumers in New York?

Doo.: Right here only a few yards away. [*To his valets.*] Bring in that Saratoga trunk and be quick about it. It's lucky we brought those togs along. [*Enter valets bearing trunk.*]

Doo.: Here they are, and whin we git inside these clothes we can do the grand in any court in Africa. [*Opens trunk and throws out all manner of court paraphernalia: trunks, tights, and the like.*] Right this way; we have the goods. [*Enter Francisera and Festicus from opposite sides of the stage. They purchase court attire from Dooley. Various characters select their wardrobes and retire.*]

Fest.: [*Eyeing Orn. suspiciously.*] I wonder if that man's a spy in Dad's employ? If I were sure I would build a head on him.[15] I wish I could find that man in the diver's suit for a few minutes.

Doo.: [*Pointing up the river.*] He's right up there, Sor. [*Fest. comes up to Dooley.*]

Fest.: Say, my boy, I want a costume that befits my station in life. I'm the Prince of Timbuctoo and have to go about disguised in these infernal checked pants.

Doo.: I have a Prince costume here with tights and a long sword and all that to be trippin' between your legs.

Fest.: Just the cheese. I will paralyze the old man when I get into the Court reception. I hear there is a San Francisco widow here in the kingdom who is bewitching the old man.

Doo.: If it's a Frisco widdy you might as well lay down. You'll see your finish soon.

Fest.: I must get in and touch him for a few million before she gets it all.

Doo.: It's a wise child that can touch his own father nowadays. [*All hands get round Dooley and his valets who hand them out the various costumes, which they take and leave the stage. Dooley and his valets finally take their own costumes, which are a lot of tights and trunks of extravagant pattern with boots that fall about the ankles. They go off the stage and soon reappear one at a time dressed in the court clothes.*]

Doo.: Well, it's blamed lucky I thought to bring these togs. We are now quite presintible and we will impress the King. Hollo, what is this? Here he comes now! [*Enter King with Francisera at his side. A portable throne is rolled in on wheels.*] Say phwat is this? He has his throne on wheels like a Vanderbilt[6] outomobile. [*Salutes the King.*] That's a fine idea ye have with the throne on wheels. Have ye it patented?

Heg.: No, any king who wants to imitate me is welcome to have one like it. [*King ascends throne with Francisera. Enter Markus, retainers, pages, heralds, counselors, etc.*] The King's Court is open. Proclaim it. [*The heralds blow blasts from their trumpets.*] Bid the Americans to my royal presence. [*Enter Orn. and the valets, followed by Zulu Lou.*]

Heg.: You saved this woman from the death she deserved. I will reward you for your heroism, but don't do it again. She hails from Zululand and no good ever came from that part of Africa. She has raised no end of trouble for my son who was quite a decent fellow until he met her. When I pass away I will cut him off without a bean. I have already banished him from the kingdom.

Mark.: [*Aside.*] That talk sounds good to me.

Lou.: [*Walking up steps of the throne.*] So you speak lightly of the Zulus. Well, the last time you tackled us we made you all take to the tall timber.

Mark.: Hold woman! You insult the King.

Lou: Oh rats! My dad holds a mortgage on the whole works. He borrowed the money to cut a swath in Paris at the Exposition,[17] eh Heggie? [*Chucks King under the chin.*]

Heg.: Away with her to the lowest dungeon. [*Guards seize her.*]

Lou: [*To guards.*] Hands off, you vermin! [*To King.*] That mortgage will be foreclosed tomorrow.

Heg.: [*To the guards.*] Don't bother about this just now. It's just a jocular way she has. Stand back, and let's see what these visitors can do. [*To Orn.*] What have you, kind sir, in the way of American novelties?

Orn.: We have brought the cathode ray, the wireless telegraph, a seismograph to record earthquakes, and an attachment to the cathode ray that enables us to read thought.[18]

Heg.: Cut them all loose at once. Does the cathode ray light up the human body?

Orn.: Yes, your majesty.

Heg.: There is a thief in my Court who has stolen some diamonds and I know he has swallowed them to avoid detection. Can you locate the jewelry?

Orn.: Absolutely. I will arrange the screen and you can pass the suspects before it. [*Arranges the screen and instrument and the King invites his Cabinet to pass before it and each pause a moment to have his picture taken.*]

Orn.: All ready.

Lou.: Look pleasant everybody. [*The members of the Cabinet pass before the screen and as they do so their stomachs appear on the screen. Finally a large fat one shows a blazing gem.*]

Heg.: Enough! Enough! Ho, guards. Take him out and bring me back the jewelry. [*Guards take him outside and the noise of the execution is heard. They return with his head on one charger and the gem on another.*]

Heg.: Ah, a cool million recovered. A clear case of what Mr. Morgan would call "undigested securities."[19] Mr. Orndorff, I make you Chief Detective of the Kingdom and from this on your salary will be half of the property you recover.

Doo.: [*To Orn.*] While he's in good humor strike him for me. I want the job of Professor of Politics and the graft of kapin' the Registry List.

Orn.: Don't butt in until I finish my stunts.

Heg.: What next? [*A ticking noise is heard.*]

Doo.: It's the wireless workin' in me trunk. Give him that next. It's news from home. [*Takes instrument from trunk and places it on the table.*] Will your majesty listen to a message from America? It's direct from the President. And addressed to you.

Heg.: Fire it out at once.

Doo.: "To the King of Timbuctoo. Greetings. Congratulations and joy for your wise reign. Will spread a plate for you at the White House next Christmas and you will eat game killed by my own hand in Cintral Park."[20] Thirty-eight words paid. Do ye want to reply?

Heg.: Certainly. "Heggamaggar to Roosevelt. Greetings." Say, what does this cost a word?

Doo.: Tin dollars.

Heg.: Well, sign my name, cut it short, and send it collect.

Doo.: Here are some Associate Press dispatches that come free. I am one of the travillin' agents of the Associate Press. [*Here can be introduced local hits with a change for each evening's performance. In case of exciting news coming over the line the finish is invariably cut off abruptly and no real news comes. The end of a horse race, prize fight, or election is always left in doubt, etc.*]

Heg.: If you can't get some definite news, why the deuce don't you hang the blamed thing up?

Doo.: The machine is so intirely sinsitive, your Highness, that every little thing butts in.

Heg.: [*Aside to his courtiers.*] Watch me have a little fun with this Irish man. [*To Dooley.*] Say, Mr. Dooley, did anyone about here ever call your attention to the remarkable resemblance your face bears to the physiognomy of the Royal Family of Timbuctoo?

Doo.: Really, your Highness, I was never put wise to that fact.

Heg.: It's certainly a very remarkable coincidence to say the least. Was your mother ever employed about the Palace?

Doo.: No, your Highness, but some years ago me father was.[21] [*Suppressed laughter about the Court checked by the heralds and guards.*]

Heg.: Have you anything else?

Doo.: Were ye spakin' of machines or ancestors?

Heg.: Produce your next American invention and hurry up.

Doo.: Let me spake to you aside. 'Tis something for your ears alone. [*Takes the King aside.*] It is the last attachment to the cathode ray and it enables you to read the hidden thoughts of yer subjects. If they are concoctin' a political job, it puts you dead next.[22] If they are plannin' to kill ye, you know it a day in advance and kapes ye from bein' the next dead. Look over the mob with this and let me know what ye see. [*Arranges instrument.*]

Heg.: [*Looking through.*] My heavens, what is this? [*The crowd cowers before the instrument.*] By the graves of my forefathers every body of any importance in the bunch is scheming to get my crown. The head of the outfit is Francisera, the favorite of my heart.

Doo.: Don't let on what you see but give 'em some smooth con talk.

Heg.: [*To the crowd.*] This is indeed a marvelous machine. I have been able to read the inmost thoughts of my faithful subjects. Each one seems to wish me a long life, a merry reign, and death at a ripe old age.

Doo.: [*Aside to King.*] That's the true business.

Heg.: Durango, as a reward for your love for me I make you Master of the Exchequer.

Durango: Thanks, your Majesty. [*Bowing low.*] Thanks.

Heg.: Askagi, I create a new office for you and it will be not unfitting to your liking. I make you Master of the Royal Harem at five thousand a year and perquisite.

Askagi: [*Bowing.*] Thanks, good King, I accept.

Heg.: Mangali, you shall guard the Royal jewels at the same price and wear them on State occasions if you like.

Mangali: [*Bowing.*] Bless you, good King. I have always loved you.

Heg.: And you Francisera, Queen of my heart, shall share the crown with me and, as I leave no heirs, succeed to my gilded throne. [*To the Head Guard.*] Did you mark well those I mentioned for my royal favors?

Guard: Yes, your Majesty. They are down upon the tablets of my memory.

Heg.: [*Aside to Dooley and Guard.*] Take them all out to the Niger and lop off their heads as fast as the posse can swing the ax. Cut Francisera's off first and tie her carcass in a sack—fit food for the fishes in the stream. She has caused one sucker to bite and now let all the suckers of the river make a meal of her. But wait a moment. I must string this cursed witch of a Zulu before she goes. When it comes to attending to her, tie her neck and heels, and weight her with plenty of rocks.

Doo.: That's right, your Majesty. Don't forgit the girl.

Heg.: [*To Lou.*] Sometimes in the past I fear I have been unkind to you not knowing your true worth. From now on you shall hold the ostrich plumes over my head when I slumber and watch my household dogs and your clothes and jewels come all from the royal exchequer. No one in all the realm shall dare dispute your milliner's bills and . . .

Lou: Can I have Festicus come home?

Heg.: Yes, child, he can return and we will kill the fatted calf.

Lou.: [*Grasping the King's hand.*] Heggie, old boy, you are the real thing. [*To crowd.*] Long live the King! [*Everybody hollers. The Court breaks into excited talk. The King has a dizzy spell, places his hand to his heart. Lou helps him as he staggers toward the throne. He falls at the foot of the throne.*]

Heg.: [*Muttering to self.*] I'm done for. They've poisoned me. The psychoscope told the truth. This is my evil hour and my last. [*Lou sits down and rests his head in her lap. To Lou.*] I really thought you the worst in the bunch but there are others I overlooked. Farewell. You held my head in my last hour and I forgive you all. Take my banished boy . . . if you can locate him. [*King dies.*]

Mark.: Stand back and give him air. Dead is he? Well, we must arrange for his funeral and his successor.

Fran.: [*Rushing forward and falling on the dead body.*] Oh mercy, mercy, is he dead? The only man I ever loved.

Lou: Rats. [*Guards lead Francisera away weeping, etc.*] She plays it pretty well.

Mark.: [*Opening big book.*] The Code of Timbuctoo places me in charge of the obsequies as Attorney General. Section six hundred and one. As he banished his son he will have to leave the Crown by will, Section one hundred and six. Does anyone happen to know of a will his Majesty has left?

Courtier: [*Advancing.*] I have one.

Mark.: Ah, the lost will! We will immediately admit it to probate.

Another Courtier.: [*Advancing.*] So have I. [*Several more advance and present wills.*]

Fran.: [*Returning and still in hysterics.*] I found this tucked under the door of my room this morning and don't know who left it there. [*Markus takes all the wills.*]

Mark.: These several documents mean a will contest and a Court Issue. Call in the Supreme Court at once and we will submit the case. Take away the body and wake up the Court Embalmer. [*Guards remove the body on a stretcher.*] Is the Court ready?

Guard: The Court is now in session. [*Pulls aside a curtain and discloses three gorillas seated behind a raised table.*]

Mark.: [*Bowing to bench.*] May it please the Court. I have several wills of his late Majesty all making different people the beneficiaries. This creates a tangle that leaves the matter for your wisdom to unravel. I suggest in such a case that the trial by fire is the only thing left. Let the gods decide. [*Cheers and shouts of approval.*] We await your answer. [*Gorillas put their heads together.*]

Center Gorilla: Several days ago we learned that the King was feeling unwell and so we looked up the authorities and acting with our usual promptness have our decision ready.[23] The trial by fire goes.

Mark.: It would have taken an American Supreme Bench two years to settle a similar case. [*A brazier of coals is brought and the ten wills cast into the flames. Francisera's will survives the ordeal and is held aloft and read by Markus.*]

Mark.: [*Reading.*] Being of sound mind and under no restraint I make this my last will and testament. Unto my beloved Francisera I give my crown, kingdom, scepter, jewels, land, gold, horses, and ivory. All other wills but this I hereby revoke and those the flames will devour. Markus, the Attorney General of the Kingdom, I appoint my sole executor without bonds. Witness my hand and seal this ___ day of ___. [*Use the date of the performance.*] Heggamaggar, King of Timbuctoo.

Crowd: Long live the Queen! Long live the Queen! [*Francisera ascends the steps of the throne and Markus places the crown upon her head.*]

Orn.: [*To Dooley.*] This bodes no good to us. What the devil were you doing all this time with my will?

Doo.: I must have got 'em mixed some way but don't be cast down. We must make the best of it now and recover later on. Profess to be her friend and sing a song of welcome.

Orn.: Yes, it's a fine time to sing songs of welcome, but I suppose now the thing has been so mixed up by your infernal blundering that I must get in and drill. Well, here goes.
[*Solo. Orn.:*]

<u>Song of Welcome</u>

Some Africa Queens are black as night,
But our good Queen is pink and white.
The top notch blood that runs in you,
Combines New York with Kalamazoo.
    Chorus:
    Then hail, Oh gracious Queen!
    The finest ever seen.
    We all adore and worship you,
    The dandy Queen of Timbuctoo.

Although you are somewhat farfetched,
Your golden scepter is outstretched.
And when you give your stern command,
You bet our foreheads hit the sand.
    Chorus.

> How dazzling are the various gems
> That deck your several diadems.
> Although the bills will soon fall due,
> Naught cares the Queen of Timbuctoo.
> *Chorus.*

[*All the people on the stage pay homage to the Queen except Zulu Lou who stands aloof and refuses obeisance.*]

Fran.: Who is this haughty maid who dares affront me in the very hour of my coronation?

Lou: I guess I'm the party and you know where to find me. [*The seismograph begins to vibrate.*]

Fran.: [*Descending from her throne in a passion.*] I'll show you the weight of a Queen's displeasure, you little hussy. [*Lifts her hands as if to strike.*]

Lou.: [*Stepping closer.*] Don't you dare swing your right at me. If you ever do I'll duck and counter. [*Snapping her fingers in the Queen's face.*] Who the deuce cares for you any how? I know how you got your title. You're a bogus brick and not a real queen. You make me tired.

Fran.: Ho, there guards! Take this wench to the darkest dungeon. [*Guards rush up and lay hold on Lou.*]

Lou: Back, all of you! The weight of your finger on me and heads will answer for it at the hands of my countrymen! [*Enter Festicus with drawn sword. He beats back the guards and hand to hand fighting follows. Lou, recovering one of the swords of a fallen guard, fights side by side with Festicus and the two advancing step by step cause the guards to retire. They then advance to the foot of the throne waving their swords in the Queen's face.*]

Fest.: I serve notice on all of Timbuctoo that I am the rightful heir to the throne and my sword will find the way.

Lou: And my sword goes with yours.

Fest.: [*Embracing her.*] My heart and hand goes with this and we will fight to the end.
[*Solo. Lou:*]

The Creature that Walks on Air

I feel like a creature that walks on air
    And things are coming my way.
Festicus is the man to dare,
    And I think he has come to stay.
His sword is dangling from his hip,
    And his fingers caress the hilt,
And nobody dares give us any lip,
    For that's not the way we are built.
    Chorus: [*Full company.*]
Festicus he comes back you see,
For he never can banished be.
Then open wide the palace door
When Festicus comes to his own once more.

She will have to fight for crown and throne,
    She'll think so before we're through.
When Festicus comes to claim his own,
    In the Kingdom of Timbuctoo.
We are good sized as Kingdoms run,
    But if you will take my cue,
There is no land lying under the sun,
    With room for ruler two.
    Chorus. [*By company.*]

End of Act First.

Act Second

Scene One

Scene. Forest near Timbuctoo. Tropical scenery, etc. On stage six pretty girls dressed as Puritan Maidens, a singing Sextet, Chaperoned by Miss Primrose, of Boston.

Enter attendants bearing wooden throne and chairs.
Prim.: Look, girls, this must be the Queen's throne, and you will see Her Majesty herself presently. [*Enter Queen Francisera, Orndorff, Dooley, Markus, and members of the Court.*]
Prim.: [*With low curtsy.*] I have a letter of introduction here, Madam, from the Mayor of Boston to any ruling Sovereign I may meet in Timbuctoo. Am I right in laboring under the impression that you are the Queen of this delightful country? [*Extends letter of introduction.*]
Fran.: [*Waving her aside, haughtily.*] Hand this to my attendant. [*Secretary steps up and takes the letter.*] Read.
Secretary: [*Reading.*] To whom it may concern. To all rulers and potentates in Africa. This will introduce to you Miss Priscilla Primrose, Chief Superintendent of the Sunday Schools of Boston, who will be with you for a short time to study the customs of your country. She is accompanied by six of her pupils. I can recommend them all as being persons of the most precise and proper character under all circumstances. You need not hesitate to introduce them to your very best society. Yours, fraternally, James Gillwicks, Mayor of Boston. By Larry Lampwicks, Clerk.

Fran.: We are very careful about receiving strangers in this country and we require the very best credentials. I am glad you took the precaution to bring this letter of introduction. I bid you welcome, and if you care to take tea with us, it will be all right.

Prim.: Permit me to thank you for your gracious invitation. Would you mind hearing my class sing something from their Sunday School selections?

Fran.: We would be only too delighted. [*Suggestions for song. The young ladies should be dressed in the costumes of Puritan Maidens. While singing each alternate line, the chaperone, Miss Primrose, should be talking to someone with her back to the sextet. The first line should be sung with great propriety with the chaperone looking on. The second, with the chaperone's back turned, should be sung with the wildest kind of dancing and high kicking, the demure air to be resumed a moment later when Miss Primrose turns her eyes to them. During the entire performance the sextet alternates between the wildest devilment and displays of "punctilious propriety"*[24] *according to the way they are being watched by the chaperone.*]

Song. [Sextet:]

When we're at home with our mammas,
    we act most circumspectly,
But when we're loose in Timbuctoo,
    we change our gait directly.
In Boston town, we never do a thing that's counted risky,
But when abroad we strike a gait that some consider frisky.
Our conduct here in Timbuctoo with levity is laden,
But in New England's clime, of course,
    we play the prudish maiden.

The way we act in Portland, Maine, is not one bit suspicious,
Which makes our little fling abroad particularly delicious.
We'll have our time in Timbuctoo, although you may be sure,
We will return to staid Vermont decidedly demure.
We pose as the perfection of punctilious propriety,
And that is why we come to go in Number One Society.
For appearing prim and proper, we have a happy faculty,
But when a little fun's afoot, we hit it with alacrity.
Therefore this observation can scarce be called a platitude,
One's moral conduct very oft is governed by the latitude.

[*During the last lines, Queen Fran. and attendants join in the song and caper about the stage dancing, all except Miss Primrose, who is very much shocked at the performance, and appears to take no stock in it.*]

Fran.: [*To the young ladies. Shaking hands with all of them in the most cordial manner.*] Say, but you folks are all right! Come right into the Palace with me and have tea. You must stop with me two weeks at least, and we'll have a genuine good time. It isn't often we have a Boston Sunday School class in Timbuctoo and when we do, I propose to make the most of it. [*To attendant.*] Come, get a move on now, mosey up to the Palace and tell the head butler that I'll have a lot of company tonight and for some weeks to come.

Prim.: This dancing and hilarity doesn't seem right to me. I'm afraid these girls will get entirely beyond my control if they remain long in this gay locality. My duties as a chaperone will be no sinecure this trip. [*Exeunt omnes. Orndorff and Dooley remain. Dooley sits tired and dejected on a log.*]

Doo.: [*To self.*] Well, everything wint wrong wid the boss, but still he's dead game. But wasn't it great nerve whin he sang that song of welcome to the new Queen?

Orn.: So you have blundered again, eh? Do you recall my instructions?

Doo.: As near as I can recollect we were to have a lot of wills tried by fire. I supposed that the will that burned with a clear blue flame would be the boss of the outfit. Well, I soaked yours with benzine and got her in with the balance. [*Orn. makes a gesture of disgust.*]

Orn.: Well, we are in a nice box, and instead of being the King of Timbuctoo, with a graft of more than a million a year, I have lost everything and am liable to have my head cut off any minute. There is one consolation, however; when my head goes, yours will go with it.

Doo.: [*Rushing up and grasping his hand.*] Thanks for those manly words. A consolation purse is better than nothing. Wid all your hard luck, Dan, I'm your friend that sticks to ye in misfortune.

Orn.: I never have anything else when with you. You are my bete noir.

Doo.: [*Excitedly.*] Now that sort of talk has gone far enough. I'm no bete noir and allow no man living to apply language like that to me. I'll overlook it this once, but I'll dust the world wid ye if ye repeat it. Stay with me and we'll yet be on top. I'll plant the flag of the Constitution here in Timbuctoo. With Chicago primary elections and post office scandals and battle ship grafts,[25] I'll make a live humming country out of this sleepy place. Say ye can trust me for that, or I will seek new alliances. [*Enter Prince Festicus.*]

Fest.: Plotting against the throne, old boy? Seeking new alliances? What do you say to joining hands with my end of the fight? I'm looking for some practical politician and I think one of the U.S. brand will be about the thing.

Doo.: [*Shaking hands.*] We'll open the game any time you say. Let me introduce me partner. [*Introduces Orn.*] He furnishes the money and I the experience. [*Orn. and Fest. shake hands.*]

Fest.: I've been tricked out of my throne by that San Francisco adventuress and I want it back. They have done away with my Father and robbed me of my inheritance.

Doo.: Why, that's easy, Prince Festicus. Dead easy. The work of reclaiming that arid throne of yours is like takin' candy from a baby. [*Enter Zulu Lou.*]

Fest.: Allow me to present my friend, Miss Zulu Lou.

Doo.: [*Grasping her hand effusively.*] Ah, Miss, that was a great fight you and your best man put up. We were speakin' of reclaiming the throne for you people, but are ye really in need of it? Wid your youth and good looks and all the world before ye, such a trifle as a throne don't seem much.

Lou: [*Indifferently.*] Well, of course as you say, one throne more or less doesn't count so much in our family, but if it isn't too much trouble you might as well cop it for us.

Doo.: Oh, of course, we'll attend to that. A good wad of money and the rest is easy.

Lou: I can get all the money you want. That's the easiest thing I know.

Doo.: Is it yer own money or are ye pullin' that young man's leg for it? Don't say no, I saw him a few minutes ago under that bamboo tree makin' love to ye and chuckin' ye under the chin. These things won't do in politics. We have no time for love makin'.

Lou: But if the right man chuckles you under the chin, I guess it's all right. Say, here comes the Queen and those precise Puritan Maidens from Boston who blew in here yesterday. They tell me that they carry Sunday School tracts and prayer books about with them and have grace said at table. Oh, but they're the limit. I believe I'll sing a risqué song for them and give them a great shock.

Doo.: Cut it loose! Now's your time. [*During the song Fran., her attendant, and the Six Maidens come in and stand behind Lou. The Sextet dance in a most abandoned manner with the music but appear perfectly staid and proper whenever she turns round to see if her words shock them.*]

[*Solo. Lou:*]
Although a bit gay I'd not have you believe,
That a woman should carry her heart on her sleeve.
So I think I'm in order when stoutly asserting,
That maidens should never be guilty of flirting.
But to qualify somewhat, I think it no sin
When the right fellow chuckles you under the chin.
  When he chuckles you, chuckles you,
   Chuckles you, chuckles you, chuckles you under
    the chin.

Of course I well know there's considerable danger,
In allowing a man who is really a stranger,
To become an acquaintance in galloping haste,
As he fondles your fingers or presses your waist.
But still there's a moment when love must begin,
If the right fellow chuckles you under the chin.
  When he etc.

But now to you maidens, particularly proper,
Who never turn handsprings without asking popper,
When back in old Boston consider it duly,
As a heart to heart talk you have had with yours truly.
Just grab at the chance if a husband you'd win.
When the right fellow chuckles you under the chin.
  When he etc.

[*During the singing of the last verse Fest. sidles up to Lou and chuckles her chin to the disgust of Orn.*]

Orn.: [*To Doo.*] Look at that familiarity with the girl I love. Shall I challenge him to mortal combat?

Doo.: Don't be a fool. We are here for politics and not any funny business like buttin' into a love affair. If we work it right we will run the politics and the finances of the kingdom and let the other fellows attend to the society business. It's that man that has the mortgage on the shanty that cuts the swath. [*Exit Fest. and Lou.*] I have a song on that line and I'm goin' to sing it right now.

[*Solo. Doo.:*]
Pat rode to see his girl upon the trolley,
The first name of his swateheart it was Molly,
And the times they had were jolly, jolly, jolly,
    Courtin' on the old back porch.

Just when the welcome shades of night were fallin',
When the nurses put the kids to bed a-bawlin',
This was Pat's appointed hour for callin',
    Round by the old back porch.

One night when Pat was very busy sparkin',
On the corner of McAllister and Larkin,
The father of his swateheart was harkin',
    Harkin' by the old back porch.

And when he heard young Pat propose to Molly,
It filled the old man's heart wid melancholy,
And with a brogan number 'leven, by Golly,
    He kicked him off the old back porch.

> But when Pat once more found his senses,
> He cursed and swore in several moods and tenses,
> And tore his pants a-climin' over fences,
> > Retratin' from the old back porch.

> Then Pat, says he, "be gorry 'tis my ante,"
> And he goes to money lender Delehanty,
> Buys up the bloomin' mortgage on the shanty,
> And now he owns the whole back porch.

Orn.: Your simple song has indeed taught me a valuable lesson and I will bide my time. Now all I want you to do is not to butt in and spoil things.

Doo.: Hist! The Queen is comin' this way and we must begin to work her. I think she is achin' to do some politics and I'll see that she gets all she wants. Lave her to me.

Fran.: [*Motioning to an attendant.*] Ask Mr. Dooley to stop this way. [*Attendant brings Doo. to Fran.*] Mr. Dooley can I have a quiet word with you for a few moments?

Doo.: My time is never too valuable [not] to give a portion to the service of your gracious Majesty. [*They come down to the center of the stage away from the rest.*]

Fran.: I suppose you know that there is a conspiracy afoot to deprive me of my right to the throne.

Doo.: I have noticed a disposition on the part of some people to make the road a trifle rocky.

Fran.: Could you straighten out my affairs with your American politics?

Doo.: Nothing easier. All you need is a vote of confidence. Submit it to a special election and I will manage the election. After that you are fixed for life.

Fran.: But suppose the election should happen to go the wrong way?

Doo.: You seem to forget, Madam, that I will supervise the election returns. I care not who makes the laws of my country if I can make the ballot boxes. [*Aside.*] The ones with the slidin' bottoms.

Fran.: All right, I will issue the election proclamation and appoint you Supervisor of Elections and if you lose the fight your head goes also.

Doo.: If you happen to run up against the Prince don't have trouble. Give him some double con talk and be friends wid him. In politics you must be smooth wid everybody. [*Exit Doo. and Orn.*]

Fran.: Wonder if I really could talk smooth to Festicus. Possibly I might on a pinch. [*Enter Fest.*] Ah, here he comes. [*Advances and offers hand cordially.*]

Fest.: I really cannot recall where we have met and I have never had the pleasure of an introduction.

Fran.: Oh, listen to me a moment. Why cannot we be friends and end this threatened strife? I shall exercise a Queen's prerogative to make the first advances. You seem to misunderstand my position here. I had met your Father in Paris and came to visit him on his invitation. He died and left everything to me. It was a mad King's freak action. At first I hesitated, but accepted the trust out of regard for you that I might later give it all to the man I loved. I took the throne that I might offer it to you.

Fest.: Oh, you did, did you? How very kind of you.

Fran.: Do not make light of my good intentions. Tomorrow I will call you to my side publicly and proclaim you . . .

Fest.: Well, go on.

Fran.: The Queen's Consort. If I may be allowed. You see I am a little new here and possibly not exactly posted on the Court marriage etiquette. Of course, if I were a mere ordinary person and not the Queen, my natural bashfulness would prevent me giving vent to the full feeling of a throbbing heart. A heart that beats alone for you.

Fest.: [*Aside.*] Natural bashfulness is good. I think I will have to give her plenty of rope. [*To Fran.*] How am I to know, an unsophisticated youth raised in the wilds of this benighted country, whether you toy with my young affections or really voice the real sentiments of a true and loving heart? Could I but believe that . . .

Fran.: [*Embracing Fest.*] Darling, may my reign end tomorrow if it continues without you. What is the jeweled scepter to me if I cannot rule your heart? Come to these waiting arms. It is the Queen who calls. The Queen who pleads for one single kiss to water the oasis of a parched and thirsty soul. Make no mistake Festicus, my love is the real thing and so am I.

[*Solo. Fest.:*]
She may press her lips to yours,
    Her arms about you cling.
Yet after all, perhaps her love
    Is not the real thing.

A score of sweethearts I recall,
    Who had me on the string,
But many of them, after all,
    Were not the real thing.
The first that made the bird of love,
    Within my heart to sing.
Was false to me and did not prove,
    To be the real thing.

The next had lovely azure eyes,
    And French could sweetly sling.
But soon she proved to my surprise,
    As not the real thing.

[*Both singing.*]
But here in dreamy Timbuctoo,
    A true devotion springs,
Your love for me and mine for you,
    Are just the real things.
[*Embrace during last verse.*]

Fran.: [*Aside.*] Oh, but he's dead easy.

Fest.: [*Aside.*] She's a smooth article sure enough, but my two winters in Paris give me some slight experience in sizing up the designing female. [*To Fran.*] I trust my heart and my future in your keeping. Never before have I met a woman whom I could trust so much. Pardon my seeming reluctance to accept your sincere declarations of affection, but you must remember that you are talking to a man who has had some sad awakenings in his young life. I have dreamed and I have wakened. This is why I hesitate.

Fran.: [*Aside.*] The woman who hesitates is lost. The man who hesitates is won. [*To Fest.*] Farewell until I make the Royal Proclamation of our betrothal. Until then we must dissemble.

Fest.: Your course is a wise one. I will follow your suggestions. Farewell. [*They embrace*]. Farewell. [*Fran. and Fest. make their exits in different directions.*]

End of Act Second, Scene One.

Scene Two

Scene. Palace of Francisera, the Queen of Timbuctoo. Interior, elevated throne. Prime Ministers, Chorus, Attendants, Pages, etc., etc. Place fitted up with seismograph, telephone, and wireless telegraph instrument. Orndorff and Dooley in the foreground.

Doo.: Well, this is the day that the bogus San Francisco adventuress will climb the throne in dead earnest. Guess we'll have to saw wood and look pleasant.

Orn.: If we allow this woman to best us, in the long run we simply deserve our fate. [*Seismograph becomes agitated.*] What's this? She must be coming. [*Blare of trumpets.*] Yes, here she comes. Let's step aside and watch the procession. [*Enter Fran. arranged in royal robes with courtiers holding screens of ostrich plumes, etc. and pickaninnies holding train.*]

Fran.: [*To pickaninnies.*] Hold that train higher you little black rascals, or I'll have your woolly heads off before sundown. [*They elevate the train.*]

Doo.: [*To Orn.*] Another mark of civilization. The elevated train.

Fran.: [*To Chorus.*] Say there, you singers, strike up some vocal music. Don't you see I'm here?

Chorus:
Here comes our gracious Queen.
Her train's the longest ever seen.
Composed of silk and velveteen,
    Of silk and velveteen.
She comes the ship of state to steer,
But still it looks a trifle queer,
Those little niggers in the rear.
    Those niggers in the rear.

The old King's hearse has passed the gate,
But still in these affairs of state,
One cannot wait, one cannot wait,
    One cannot wait.
Old King Heggamaggar is dead and gone.
And now a new regime is born.
So let's all dance upon the lawn,
    Dance lightly on the lawn.

She stands now in the dead King's shoes.
She is the ruler that we choose,
So start the music, tap the booze,
    Turn loose the merry booze.
She is both beautiful and young,
So give the flaring trumpet tongue,
Roll out the cask and start the bung,
    Be sure and start the bung.

Fran.: Thanks everybody for those kind works of cheer. I want you to all to understand that I am in for a long reign and a merry one. Now everybody have one with me. [*Lifts goblet.*] But, hold on. Where are the girls from Boston? They don't seem to be here and I don't want them to miss any of the fun. [*Sound of laughter in the distance.*] Oh, here they come. They had tea with me and then they tapered off on something stronger. [*Enter Sextet of Puritan Maidens dressed in short skirts followed by Miss Primrose.*]

Prim.: Oh, this is awful. Simply awful. Look at those clothes. And to think of my Sunday School class.

Fran.: They are right in the fashion now and when ladies travel abroad they should adopt the prevailing fashions of each country they travel in.

Song. Sextet:
Some people think that we are flirts,
Because we wear these shortened skirts.
We have to be in fashion's swim,
And if it shows an ankle trim.
[*They dance.*]

We hope no one will make a fuss,
Or find the slightest fault with us.
We wear our dresses at the knees.
Because of fashion's stern decrees.
[*Dance.*]

We dress so high above the shoe,
Because the Queen of Timbuctoo,
Has said that we must dress that way,
And therefore we obey, obey.
For latest modes we have to lean,
On the caprices of the Queen,
If scantier clothes she should decree,
We wouldn't cross the Queen. Not we.

Fran.: Thanks awfully for that song. Now to business. I wish to announce that it is my royal will that we have a general election on the fifteenth of this month, which is the second Tuesday in October. Heretofore you have been denied the right of suffrage. I now give it to you on a platter. [*Cheers.*] I hereby appoint Mr. Dooley, late of Chicago, as my Inspector of Elections. Mr. Dooley, advance and receive your commission. [*Immense document with dangling seals, etc.*]

Doo.: Thanks, your Majesty. I will guard the ballot box wid me life and wear this commission next me heart.

Fran.: Daniel Orndorff of New York, I appoint you my Secretary of State. Advance and tell me truly if you are a Buffalo.[26] [*Orn. advances.*]

Orn.: I accept your commission and will add that it is a long time since I looked upon so fair a queen.

Fran.: All loyal members of the late king's household I appoint in a body at an advance of salary. The Treasury is bursting with money and we may as well proceed to rake it. [*Herald announces the arrival of a messenger from the United States.*] From America? Admit him. [*Enter a young man in the dapper costume of a drummer*[27] *and, reaching the throne, hands out a document.*] Ah, I see. A bill of one million dollars and upward for diamonds against the late lamented King Heggamaggar. Yes, some of the presents he made me in Paris. [*To Collector.*] This bill is against the late King. You will find him in the Elephant Hill Cemetery, fifth grave to the left with a big boulder on top. I suppose I'll have to settle this anyhow. Here, Master of the Exchequer, bring in the strong box and settle this bill. [*Master of Exchequer blows whistle and attendants enter bearing a strong box heavily padlocked. To Collector.*] Here young man, receipt this bill at once.

Collector: But I can't until I have the money.

Fran.: Oh indeed, can't you? Ho! Guards. [*Enter three guards who grab Collector and are about to behead him.*] Show this youngster how to receipt that bill. [*Collector receipts bill.*]

Members of Sextet: Oh, isn't that perfectly lovely! How I wish some of those New York milliners would come over here. The Queen's business methods are just too cute for anything. [*The strong box is here opened and the Master of the Exchequer turns it upside down and jumps on it. Thirty cents fall out and are handed over to Collector.*]

Collector: Heavens! How can I return without the money?
Fran.: Don't have to return. Stay here and spend the summer with us. You never would regret it and we would give you the time of your life.

    Song. [*Sextet and Chorus:*]
We stretch the good glad hand to you,
We're sure you'll never, never rue,
A summer spent in Timbuctoo.
    In Timbuctoo, In Timbuctoo.
      'Buctoo, 'Buctoo.

[*Collector sings:*]
From gay New York I've come straight through,
To land my trunk in Timbuctoo.
Chorus:
    In Timbuctoo, In Timbuctoo.

I've seen the sights of gay Paree,
But this town is the place for me.
Chorus:
    The place for me. The place for me.

Although I do not mean offense,
What can I do with thirty cents?
Chorus:
    With thirty cents? With thirty cents?

Just guessing roughly off the reel,
It indicates the way I feel.
Chorus:
    The way we feel. The way we feel.

> Although I'd like to get me hence,
> One can't go far on thirty cents.
> *Chorus:*
> > You can't go far on thirty cents. [*Repeat.*]

Collector casts money at foot of throne.

Fran.: [*Picking up money.*] I see it's high time to economize. I'll save this for pin money. Somebody has looted the Royal Treasury of several dollars and I will have to levy some more taxes. [*Aside.*] I must, however, play politics first and conciliate all my enemies. [*Enter Festicus and Zulu Lou.*] My Royal welcome to you, Prince Festicus. [*Descends throne and extends hand.*] I hereby lift the ban of banishment and bid you thrice welcome to our Court. [*Sextet girls and others crowd about the Prince and extend hilarious welcome.*]

Lou: [*Advancing saucily.*] Well, how about me?

Fran.: [*Advancing as the seismograph begins to gyrate.*] I want you to make yourself mighty scarce about the Court. If I catch you here again there'll be work for the headsman.

Lou: Oh, go get the ax. [*Snapping her fingers in the Queen's face.*] Not one of your gang dare lay a hand on me and you know it.

> [*Solo. Lou:*]
> Just be careful what you do,
> When you fool with Zulu Lou,
> For I do not care a fig,
> When the Queen is on her dig.
> > I'm a comer. I'm a hummer, all the same.
> I still the secret hold,
> Where the dead King canned his gold.
> And that's the reason why,
> You never dared deny,
> > I'm a comer. I'm a hummer. Roll your game.

> For my dad's in sole command,
> Of the troops of Zululand.
> And a hundred thousand spears,
> Will come buzzing round your ears,
>   If you ever lay a hand upon this chile.
> They would make short work of you,
> All you guys of Timbuctoo.
> They would mow you down like grass,
> If you gave them any sass.
>   They are comers. They are hummers, all the while.

Fran.: [*Aside.*] If she knows where the King's sack is we must take her into camp at once. [*To Lou.*] You sing most charmingly, my dear. Your voice has quite captivated me, with its velvet vocalization and its extraordinary technique.

Lou: Possibly the words also had their effect. If you want to get your hands on any of that swag, you must cotton to me and also make things pretty comfortable for the Prince. I hope I make myself understood. If you want to know any more about my affairs, talk to my attorney.

Doo.: She'll have a nice time getting anything out of him. They all know how to kape mum. Lawyers, priests, and Frinch restaurant waiters. All in the same lodge. [*Fran. advances toward Lou when the clicking of the wireless telegraph instrument is heard.*] What's that? A message from America. Come here everybody and git the news. [*Reads from slip.*] Great International Yacht race. This is the finish. Boats only four feet apart. Sir Thomas Lipton bets a million.[28] Hurrah! The head yacht wins.

Fran.: Which is the head yacht? I had a small stake on that myself.

Doo.: The wireless don't say, but it's telling of a big prize fight at Carson City, Nevada.[29] For the championship of the world. It's the last round and a man is bein' counted out.

Prim.: Which man? I'm dying to know!

Doo.: The machine don't mention his name, but it says the excitement there is intense. But keep quiet. There's a big primary going on in my ward in Chicago and me friend Hennessey is down the Potter Palmer gang.[30] Oh hang the blasted machine! It says that one gang has won out by a four hundred and fifty-nine majority, but it don't say which one! I was about to git the names of the winners, when this dispatch telling how Teddy Roosevelt was about to bag a trust, has broke in on me!

Prim.: Did it say which trust Teddy bagged?

Doo.: It didn't mention which one. We can get the name of the first trust he bags by slow freight and it'll be just as well. But here's word from Rev. Joel McWhacker. He says to make the announcement that he will hold religious services in the South End Church tommorry morning and in the North End Church in the afternoon and in the evening children will be. . . . There. It quits again.

Lou: I suppose he wants to say that in the evening children will be baptized at both ends.

Doo.: That'll do for you, Miss Zulu Lou.

Fran.: Hang the wireless telegraph. We never get any news anyhow. Cut it out and let's have some sort of diversion. What's the matter with an American cakewalk?[31] [*To the Sextet.*] Can you give us an American cakewalk?

Prim.: How dare you ask my Sunday School scholars to do a thing like that! We don't have such things in Boston society as vulgar cakewalks.

One of the Sextet: We don't, huh? Well you just watch us. [*Music strikes up and cakewalk begins. After the cakewalk, with Miss Primrose dancing the last steps, there is great applause from the natives. In response to an encore, Prim. dances one all by herself. She dances more extravagantly than all the rest, etc.*]

Fran.: All this is very diverting and from this on I want a cakewalk at all the royal functions. But to have something stirring here, how would you like a sword contest? [*Looks toward Fest.*]

Fest.: I stand ready to meet all comers with the foils. [*Glances in the direction of Orn.*] I hear that the United States boasts of some good swordsmen. Possibly it may have some worthy representative here.

Doo.: Dan, he names you. Git out your sticker and tackle him.

Orn.: [*Advancing toward Fest.*] I am at your service. [*Salutes.*]

Fran.: [*Taking Fest aside.*] Now is the supreme hour for you to show me how well you love me. In your bout with this American, let the stakes be Zulu Lou. Let him win the girl and it will clear the way for our union. You lose a dusky forest girl and win me and a throne.

Fest.: [*Aside.*] So, so. I am to lose Lou and win the Queen. She's playing her usual bold game with her usual nerve. Well, I'll dissemble some more. I'll throw the match, eh? No. I'll win and give all hands the double cross. [*To Fran. and all.*] Well, your Majesty, what shall the prize be in this trial of our skill? Can your Majesty name the stakes? I never measure swords with any man except for something worth the while.

Orn.: So you fight for money, eh? I thought your father, in his life time, was well to do?

Fest.: On the contrary, I found him devilish hard to do. But still they managed to do him.[32] [*To Fran.*] Will your Majesty name the stakes?

Fran.: I select the greatest prize that I can bestow upon a gallant victor. I name the fair maid of Timbuctoo, late of Zululand. [*Both salute Fran.*]

Doo.: This is indeed a great stake and by the powers, I challenge the winner. Choose your corners. Principals, take their positions and salute.

[*Solo. Fest.:*]
    <u>My Sword Shall Find the Way</u>

One who would win an African maid,
Must press his suit with supple blade.
While love shall hold its sway,
My sword shall find the way.
      My sword shall find the way.

I meet my foe in forest shade,
With hilt to hilt and blade to blade.
He goes to certain doom today.
And this good sword shall show the way.
      This sword shall show the way.
Orn. Sings:
If 'twere not for this Zulu Lou,
I would not measure swords with you,
When death claims you for his own,
Her smiles will be for me alone.
      Will be for me alone.

[*They fight, Orn. getting a slight advantage.*]

Fest.:
With thrust and parry, carte and tierce,[33]
We close in the encounter fierce.

[*As the fighting is resumed Orn. is getting a decided advantage when Doo. rushes in and grabs his sword arm.*]

Doo.: Hurrah, hurrah! I've just got a wireless from Chicago and my friend Hennessey has downed the Potter Palmer gang. [*Orn. misses his parry because of the interruption and falls wounded.*]

Fest.: [*Standing over his fallen adversary.*]
The dog has had his day.
My sword has found the way.

[*Walking toward the Queen and saluting.*] I have won the contest and claim the prize.

Orn.: [*Rising. To Doo.*] You cursed idiot. I would have won, but you butted in. [*The seismograph begins to vibrate violently and the pickaninny attendants, seeing it in motion, drop everything and take to their heels.*]

Fran.: [*Coming down off her throne and quaking with rage as she addresses Fest.*] So I have been given the double cross. There's high treason here and somebody will sweat for this. You are both under the ban. I hereby make the edict of banishment issued by your father perpetual and my royal curse goes with it.

Lou: [*Walking up to Fran.*] Oh, rats! Who cares a rap for your curse? Now come off the perch. You fixed up a job to get Festicus away from me. If you ever get him you have to fight me and I tell you, Frankie, I'm a bad one when I get excited.

Fran.: A Queen cannot dirty her royal hands on such trash as you. Ho, guards! Ho, guards!

Lou: [*Mocking her.*] Ho, guards! Hear that! Bring on your guards and I'll pay 'em their long due salary. [*Struts about the stage and snaps her fingers at the guards as they come in.*]

[*Solo. Fran:*]
Must I forget my dignity,
To notice her malignity.
    And make my court the butt of all the earth?
Must I leave my regal throne,
Perchance to pick a bone,
    With this poor jade of lowly Zulu birth?

> Must I lay aside my crown,
> To put this hussy down,
> > And make my court the scorn of Timbuctoo?
> Must I slap this saucy mouth,
> That comes vaunting from the south?
> > I guess that's just exactly what I'll do.

[Slaps Lou's mouth. Guards rush in between before Lou can retaliate.]
Fest.: The first guard who lays a finger on her dies. [*Guards rush upon him. He fights them back when Orn. rushes in to his defense. The two beat back the guards. To crowd.*] On the fifteenth of the month there will be an election here to decide whether this bogus brick shall still occupy the throne or me, the rightful heir. I appeal to my countrymen to back me at the polls.
Orn.: [*Advancing to his side.*] Good boy, Festy! I'm with you.

> *Fest.:*
> Let those who oppose may,
> My sword will find the say.

> *[Chorus and Sextet:]*
> His sword shall find the way.
> > His sword shall find the way.

> *[Curtain.]*

End of Act Second.

Act Third

Scene One

Scene. Front: Forest near Timbuctoo. On stage Orndorff and Dooley together.

Orn.: Well, I have to thank you again for butting in at the very moment when you could do the most damage. But for your infernal blundering I would have killed my man.

Doo.: A merciful interposition of providence. The news I got set me wild. I couldn't help it. Had you killed Festicus, we would have both been lynched. It was great the manly way you came to the center at the wind up.

Orn.: My feeling for fair play carried me away.

Doo.: It was great politics. Andrew Carnegie has just sent me a wireless to get in line with the Prince and we must obey orders.

Orn.: What's your plan?

Doo.: We will introduce real Philadelphia politics here and carry the election wid the moral weight of plenty of greenbacks. But I'll corrupt nobody. I'll use stage money whin I buy votes.

Orn.: I think myself that it's a good idea to use that box of green goods that man gave us on the steamer coming over. It won't be corrupting them as much.

Doo.: It won't be corruptin' 'em at all.

Orn.: Well, you know we have two boxes of campaign arguments. One, the counterfeit variety and the real thing in case of emergency—in case the voters repudiate the first.

Doo.: I'll take both boxes in case of emergency. [*Orn. retires and brings in two boxes, which he hands to Doo.*] Number one the real thing and number two the stage effect currency.

The fiat money, so to speak. Oh, I did great work in the registration business. I just took what they had. Gold dust, ivory, elephant hides, coconuts and any old thing. I let all the chimpanzees over eight years old come in and they paid the fee in coconuts. This is what I call universal suffrage wid the bark on. Today I'll open the sack at both ends and make our party popular with the people. The sturdy yeomanry, their country's pride. Wait 'til I git the ballot box and show ye. [*Exit Doo.*]

Orn.: What an enthusiasm and hopefulness he has. With all his faults, I like him. And besides, I think he'll win the fight for me. [*Enter Doo. dragging a ballot box on wheels. Big dry goods box.*]

Doo.: Here is the thing itself. This box will receive the yeomen's ballots fallin' like the driven snow. But not fallin' in price. Holloa! Look here! [*Enter Zulu Lou.*]

Lou: Say Dooley is that the ballot box? If it is, I want to vote today and at the same time, Mr. Orndorff, I want to thank you for standing in with Festicus and me in that mix-up we had. You are all right. [*They shake hands.*]

Doo.: You wimmin kin vote if ye agree to put 'em in right. I am always leery of wimmin suffrage since the Dimmicrats of Colorady giv the wimmin the ballot.[34] Were the creatchers grateful? Not much! They turned in and swept the Dimmicratic Party off the earth in that state. That was the ind of wimmin suffrage all over the Union. No party dare trust the misguided wimmin after that. A burnt kid dreads the fire.

Lou: I don't care a rap what those women did in Colorado. I have a bunch of votes here in my grip and I want to vote 'em. They are forninst the administration.

Doo.: You're just in time, you swate thing. [*Opens the lid.*] I'll be lightin' my pipe while you exercise the precious heritage, the Heaven-given right of suffrage. [*Turns and lights his pipe while Lou dumps several large armfuls of ballots into the box, climbs in and stamps on them with both feet.*] Have ye deposited yer vote, Miss?

Lou: Yes. I put in one . . . [*Aside*] . . . armful . . . [*To Doo.*] and one for the Prince.

Doo.: The vote for the Prince should have been put in by himself personally, but as ye may be unused to the proper methods I overlook the triflin' irregularity. Well, so long, Miss. I must take the ballot box now to the pollin' place and give some of the rest of the voters a show. [*Exit Doo. with ballot box.*]

Lou: Well, I wonder if I didn't get a few ballots in? This is my first attempt and I think I did fairly well for a starter. [*Enter Festicus.*] Oh, is that you? [*They embrace.*] How goes the election?

Fest.: Dooley has just opened the polls and the excitement is tremendous. I never saw anything like it.

Lou: Say, Festy, I voted.

Fest.: What! Do women vote at this election?

Lou: [*Whispering.*] Say, don't give it away. I put in ten thousand against the measly old Queen.

Fest.: [*Embracing her.*] Say, but you are surely all right. You are simply a peach. Getting in with that young printer's devil was great work! He certainly landed the goods.

Lou: Dooley tells me that the Queen is a regular tough from San Francisco. And they say a San Francisco adventuress is simply the limit. Didn't Orndorff act splendid? If we win we'll invite him to the blowout.

Fest.: Lou, do you know I dreamed of you last night?

Lou: Tell me all about it.

[*Duet. Lou and Fest.*]
Fest.:
I dreamed that I walked in the forest shade,
  Where the mottled sunlight shone.
I was the man and you the maid,
  And we wandered on alone.
The sunset sank in the gilded west,
  And the shadows of twilight fell,
But the love in your heart was all confessed,
  If pleading eyes could tell.
    When will my dream come true?
    I ask the fates as I ask of you,
    When will the dream of my life come true?
    When will my dream come true?

Lou:
I dreamed that I walked by the restless sea,
  'Neath glorious autumn skies,
But the glow of the sunset was lost to me,
  In the light of your tender eyes.
A chilling wind had wrapped me round,
  But I did not feel the blast,
For in your warm embrace I found,
  A haven of rest at last.
    When will my dream come true?
Fest.:
I seemed to wander in foreign climes,
  Away from dear Timbuctoo,
But the winds like the murmur of distant chimes,
  Brought tidings of love from you.

The twilight ebbed its life away,
    And the stars began to shine,
But the light in my heart was the light of day,
    For you told me you would be mine.
        When will my dream come true?

Lou:
The storm clouds gathered from far and near,
    And the thunder broke above,
But the roar of the breakers I did not hear,
    While you whispered your words of love,
The tongue of the tempest lapped the sea,
    And the lightnings laced the west,
But the whole wide world seemed calm to me,
    As I lay in your arms at rest.

Both:
    Now has our dream come true,
    You tell to me as I tell to you,
    How the sweetest dream of a life comes true,
    How the dream of our lives comes true.

[*Enter Orn. right.*]

Orn.: [*Aside.*] There they are, locked in each other's arms while I am on deck doing the politics which gives them the throne and happiness and leaves me quite in the soup. Well, I am a programmer from way back and I voted according to program. Thus has politics always served me. [*Enter Doo. with his eye blacked and his clothes torn.*]

Orn.: Have the polls opened yet?

Doo.: Well, I should say they have.

Orn.: Have you voted?

Doo.: No sir, I was too late. A big gorilla from the sixth precinct had already voted on my name. The Queen has been colonizin' whole districts wid monkeys, chimpanzees, and apes and I stood the raw work for the sake of party harmony. But they crowded me too far and I opened a roughhouse.[35]

Orn.: What started you?

Doo.: They voted a Chinaman and this started me feelin' beyond the calm control of reason. "It shall never be," said I, "that the Heathen of the Orient shall place their sacrilegious hands on the unpolluted palladium of American liberty,"[36] and wid that remark I socked him a good right hand jolt under the ear. Then the riot commenced and two gorillas landed on top of me and I only bate them off with difficulty. I had to ring in some of this new fangled Jetsey Jitsu[37] work from Japan to be able to git away at all.

Fest.: Tell me, Dooley, how do things really look for our cause?

Doo.: They look mighty bad the way things is goin'. [*Enter Messenger.*]

Mess.: The Queen's forces are carrying everything. Voting hundreds from the Ijiji[38] district over and over again.

Doo.: Heavings! It's like a Chicago primary.

Mess.: All the monkeys in the Passamonia district have voted twice already.

Doo.: Universal suffrage with a vengeance. Any more Chinamen?

Mess.: Here comes another messenger on the dead jump. [*Enter Second Mess.*]

Second Mess.: We need a wad of money right quick in the eighth ward.

Doo.: Here, take this box of greenbacks and cut it loose. [*Gives out box. Mess. takes it. Exit Mess.*]

Orn.: We may need the real money before we get through.

Doo.: Heaven protect me, but that bat I got in the eye must have addled my brain. I guv out the wrong box!

Orn.: Of course, it wouldn't have been you if you hadn't. I'd like to bat the other eye for you!

[*Song. Lou:*]
Mr. Dooley, tell me truly.
> Just how goes the voting?
Do you note the fleeting vote,
> Mostly known as "floating"?

Fighting, bluffing, ballot stuffing.
> How are things a-goin'?,
Roughs and heelers, and the squealers,
> Calling for their coin.

Mr. Dooley, tell me truly,
> How are things a-lookin'?
Has the broth all kinds of froth,
> With many people cookin'?

Doo.: Come now, Miss, let up on the singin'. We have no time for such nonsense. We want gold notes, if anything, in this kind of a fight.

Lou: Is it money you need, Dooley? I alone can furnish it. I alone hold the secret of the dead King's gold. Crawl down in that big hollow tree just back of the summer hacienda and there you'll find it. Help yourself. There's a little door to open and here's the key. [*Takes key from her bosom and hands it to Doo.*]

Doo.: Bless you my child, the day is won. In the bright dixshinnery of youth there's no such word as fail. [*Exit Dooley.*]

Orn.: [*Extending his hand to Fest.*] Politics, they say, makes strange bedfellows. We were seeking each other's lives not long ago and now we are on the same side of a political fight. I am a regular programmer and it's in the program for you to succeed this bogus Queen. You can count on my support until the end.

Fest.: Well spoken, young man, and here's my hand. [*Shake.*]

Lou: And here's mine. [*Shake.*] The key of the fight is that key I just gave Dooley. It's all off but the shoutin' after he gets into that strong box.

Orn.: I have never before realized what a power a woman could be in politics until today. [*Cheers in the distance.*] What's this? [*Enter crowd of people shouting and bringing in the ballot box.*]

Doo.: [*To Lou.*] At the last minute I dumped tin thousand of that money in and it relieved the situation. We will win sure. Oh, but you're a darlin'. That ballot box looks as if it had been through a hard battle. [*To crowd.*] Here, give me that box and I will take charge of it as Supervisor of Elections and place me seal on it according to law. [*Seals it.*]

Mark.: Under the law, you must sleep on it overnight. Section six hundred and one.

Doo.: I have a tired feeling right now and I'm ready to go to bed. [*Stretches himself on the box and snores.*]

Fest.: Well, it's getting late and I think we can all retire with the best of feeling and wait until the official count tomorrow. [*Exeunt omnes. Enter Queen Francisera.*]

Fran.: [*To self.*] I wonder what the result is? I guess I'll throw a cathode ray through that box and see what's on the inside. [*Arranges instrument and turns on the light. On the screen behind Doo. shines out the inscription, "Queen loses by 9999 majority."*] Oh Heavens! All is lost! Why did not fate spare me this unhappy hour? [*Faints.*]

Doo.: [*Talking in his sleep.*] Well, I think we put it all over the bogus Queen! [*Fran. rouses and listens.*] We've done her good and brown today.

Fran.: What do I hear? This man a traitor and one of my appointments? He sleeps. It may be the ravings of a disordered stomach. I cannot believe him false. [*Throws ray on Dooley's stomach.*] I will see what the instrument reveals. [*Large black crow disclosed on the screen.*] What a crow! He must have eaten this unwholesome bird with all the feathers on. No wonder he's ravin' in his dreams.

Doo.: [*Still asleep.*] Whin we count the votes I guess it'll surprise her Majesty somewhat.

Fran.: On the contrary, I'll surprise you somewhat! I'll show these people that knowledge is power. I'm the wrong woman to monkey with this time. That black bird in Dooley's stomach is a bird of evil omen to them all. I'll strike now for the throne. I'll put the whole gang in jail and I'll postpone the count until I am ready to count. I have the District Attorney Markus on my side and if you have the District Attorney on your side in an election count you don't need anything else. I'll have vengeance and I'll have blood. [*Exit Queen.*]

Doo.: [*Waking up.*] I had a terrible dream or I heard a queer noise. I dreamt the Queen was goin' to revive the ancient custom of havin' a human barbecue. If she does, we're cooked, that's all!

[*Enter Miss Primrose with Sextet finding Doo. seated dejectedly on the ballot box with torn clothes, black eye, and looking generally done up.*]

Doo.: What do all you people want?

Prim.: You look tired, Mr. Dooley.

Doo.: This infernal election would tire anybody. If they make such roughhouse at the start, what will they do later on?

Prim.: I think you made a serious mistake when you failed to get us on your side. We legged all day—I mean we pulled all day for the Queen.

Doo.: I guess you mean that you pulled the Queen's leg all day. I don't go a cint on female suffrage.

        Song. Sextet:
How do you do? How do you do,
Mr. Dooley-ooley-oo?
How does it seem? How does it seem,
To waken from your dopey dream?
To find how quickly you are through,
With politics in Timbuctoo.

Mr. Dooley-ooley-oo,
How does the contest look to you?
What makes you seem so sad?
Why do you feel so bad?
Just because you couldn't do,
The dandy Queen of Timbuctoo?
        Yours truly,
          Mr. Dooley-ooley-ooley-ooley-oo.

Doo.: This is a nice hour of the night for you people to be gallivantin' about the country. I'm surprised at your costume, Miss Primrose.

Prim.: The Queen has commanded short skirts for all of us and I'm merely obeying the mandates of fashion. As for being up late at night, it's customary to remain up all night and watch the returns. Beside that, we are having a good time and we don't want to go to bed. [*Enter Fest., Lou, Orn., Mark.*]

Lou: How has it gone? The Queen's side is already celebrating and the palace is a scene of revelry. How do they know they've won before the votes are counted? [*Enter Officer.*]

Doo.: That's the regular thing. It's only a big bluff. Sometimes it's best to have your jag before the votes are counted, for after the count you won't want any hilarity. [*To Officer.*] But who are you, Sor?

Off.: I have some warrants to serve. I am here to place a number of you people under arrest. Festicus, Zulu Lou, Mr. Orndorff, Mr. Dooley, you are all under arrest.

Doo.: And the charge, please?

Off.: False registration, conspiracy, ballot stuffing, fraudulent voting, falsifying the returns of election, embracery, and high treason.

Lou: Have you left out anything?

Off.: The Grand Jury is in session and they may find some more counts in a few days.

Orn.: And what is the penalty for all this?

Mark.: Section one thousand and one. Code of Timbuctoo. You will all be cooked after the most approved methods and eaten. There will be a human barbecue to which all the best people will be invited. The Queen is desirous of playing to the gallery a little and by returning to the ancient cannibalistic rites of the forefathers of the Empire once more get on deck politically. The natives who have learned of the Queen's plan are crazy with delight. Gilt-edged invitations to the blow-out will be circulated in a few days among the four hundred of Timbuctoo.[39]

Orn.: We have dug our political and actual graves. This is the end. Nothing but bad luck all my life. The ill wind always fans me with its breath.

[*Solo. Orn.:*]

<u>The Ill Wind</u>

There is a wind which blows across life's plain,
    To some blows good, to some blows ill,
To some it comes as music's sweetest strain,
    To me so cold and chill.

> Why does the wind through all these weary years,
>   That sweeps across the brine,
> Bring freighted argosies to line your piers,
>   And shattered wrecks to mine?
>
> But when fate drops the distaff and the skein,
>   And life no more allures,
> Perchance the wind will sing as sweet a strain,
>   Above my grave as yours.

Doo.: For Heaving's sake, Dan. Don't turn loose such doleful ditties as that just because we are in a hold. I may blunder and butt in and make mistakes but one has never accused Dooley, Prisident of the Sixth Ward Club, Chicago, of losing his nerve.

Prim.: That's right, Mr. Dooley, and we all like you for it. I don't think you are being treated exactly right. They may cook and eat every one of you but I will say right here that unless they have some regular Boston baked beans at this barbecue, I for one shall not grace the occasion with my presence.

Doo.: Thanks for these kind words and I would make bold to ask you if you can give us something livelier in the way of music to offset this last doleful melody of me friend Orndorff.

Prim.: Possibly you could give us something yourself, Mr. Dooley. Just to show your good nerve in this painful hour.

Doo.: I'm dead game to do it, all right, if this Officer will consider me out on bail for a few minutes.

[*Solo. Doo.:*]

Upon the Foreign Beach

> While strolling on the foreign beach,
>   You see some funny sights,

That used to be beyond our reach,
    Likewise beyond our rights.
'Til Uncle Sam got greed for gold,
    Combined with longer reach,
And now we grab all we can hold,
    Upon the foreign beach.
Chorus:
As we stroll upon the beach,
    After the battle's won,
We hear the verdict from all sides,
    How well the trick was done.
If we but land in proper style,
    Some good will come to each,
When our brave soldiers take a stroll,
    Upon some foreign beach.

We sent our ships across the sea,
    Our ways and creeds to teach,
We stand the natives up in line,
    And then annex the beach.
In fact we do a lot of things,
    We didn't used to do,
Until our flag's protection flings,
    O'er harems in Sulu.
Chorus.

End of Act Third, Scene One.

Scene Two

Scene. Forest. Queen Francisera's throne at left. Arrangement for a feast. Great gathering of people. Large kettles hanging from tripods. Natives bringing wood. Orndorff, Festicus, Zulu Lou, Dooley, Markus, and full Court with Sextet and Chorus. Sextet dressed in tights led by Miss Primrose who has the scantiest clothes of all. Orn., Doo., Fest., and Lou as prisoners in the foreground. Time: close to sundown.

Fran.: [*To prisoners.*] Well, the time has arrived when under the law we count the ballots. As you people have, however, already been convicted and sentenced to death for interfering in the quiet and peace of our elections, the formality of counting the ballots will have to be dispensed with. [*Cheers by the natives.*] You must by this time perceive the futility of introducing American methods into Timbuctoo politics. Some people might ask you if you had anything to say before passing from this naughty world into the oblivion of the next. Console yourselves, however, with the reflection that while you get your just deserts we will also get ours and you will be well served—by the finest chefs in the entire Kingdom. I have, however, decided to allow you a little recreation before you die. I have prepared a particularly gorgeous sunset which you can see without charge. It is the last one you will ever gaze on and you had better not overlook any of its beauties. [*As Fran. speaks, a beautiful sunset spreads over the sky in the background. This scene should be managed with stereoscopic effects and changed every night. It can be advertised as the actual sunset of the day of the performance. Golden sunsets, red sunsets, gray, or storm effects managed by mingling of different colored scenes. The idea is to make the sunsets very realistic and spectacular, gradually fading away as the play proceeds. The scene to be followed by an eclipse of the moon, which is supposed to be also as realistic as possible, a spectacular exhibition which will tax the stage effects of the theater.]*

Fest.: Whatever comes, we will face our fate with brave hearts. We will chant our death song and die.

Quartette. Fest., Orn., Doo., and Lou:

Beyond Timbuctoo's cedars,
The sun god's fleeting leaders,
    With foaming flanks and fading beyond the shadows fly.
The wind-stirred mountain vapors,
In wild fantastic capers,
    Throw gray and mottled shading upon the western sky.

But now the scene so prosy,
Lights up with colors rosy,
    And when the stars have twinkled with an
    opalescent hue,
The sky is strewn with patches,
Of sanguinary splashes,
    Like blood of day just sprinkled on the
    omnipresent blue.
Now comes a golden glowing,
Like harvest after sowing,
    And all the heavens are shining and gleaming
    in the west.
Now seen with mellow tinges,
And green and yellow fringes,
    Those golden curtains lining the palaces of rest.

But now in masses vastly,
The clouds grow dim and ghastly,
   With all the scene dissolving in pale dissembling mist.
Farewell, thou faint memorial,
Of colors purgatorial,
   Oh skies at parting, glowing with trembling amethyst.

Fran.: Let the Herald proclaim the doom of the accused.

Herald: All the defendants mentioned in the complaint as having conspired against the Queen are condemned to die. May the Lord have mercy on their worthless souls. It is further decreed that they be fed to the populace that the ancient rites of our forefathers may be revived. [*Cheers by the natives.*]

Fran.: If you people desire to bid each other farewell you are at liberty to do so—provided, of course, that you do not waste too much valuable time.

Doo.: [*To Fran.*] I think I'll take advantage of your kind offer to spake a few words of consolation to me associates and sind a farewell wireless dispatch to me old friend Hennessey.

Fran.: You are at liberty to gratify your whim, but be quick about it.

Doo.: [*To Orn.*] Say old fellow, cheer up. I have dropped on a scheme to get out of this scrape and win hands down. [*Pulls an almanac from his pocket.*] Do ye see this? It's an almanac and it shows there will be a total eclipse of the moon here tonight and it's due in a few minutes. When the time is ripe, I will announce that if a hair of our heads is hurt we will darken the face of the moon and bring about the end of the world. This will paralyze the superstitious natives and I will also wire me friend Hennessey in Chicago to sind a wireless at the nick of time and we'll scare the packin' out of these people. It's the only card left to play, but we'll play it.

Orn.: It looks good, Dooley, but I don't think you can even manage an eclipse without some blunder.

Doo.: These are unkind words, Dan, but I'll be magnanimous. I'll give ye the eclipse. Take it. It's all yours. It's due in tin minutes and I must git a move on. First, here goes to Hennessey. No one here can read it as the message will be wound off the tape in Chicago, but the answer will be printed on the tape here and the Queen will have the natural curiosity to read it. [*Goes to wireless instrument and sends message.*] There, it's gone, and I have sent it to the Criterion saloon where Hennessey is always found at this hour solving the great social and political problems of the nation. I told him to say that the world was comin' to an end tonight and sign President Roosevelt's name to it.

Fran.: Any more farewells? Time presses and my people are waiting.

Doo.: May it please your Majesty, I have a few remarks to make before I allow this little game to go any further. I have a little surprise in store for you people. A few minutes ago ye were kind enough to trate us to a very fine exhibition of a sunset. We all appreciate your generosity in tratin' us to a spectical that didn't cost ye a dime. I always liked a free show. Not to be outdone, we shall do as much for you. We will give ye an exhibition in a few minutes that will make yer hair curl. We will darken the face of the moon. You see it now? [*Pointing to the rising moon in its full.*] It looks as fine as a Bryan silver dollar,[40] but after we give it a swat wid our magic power, the mighty orb of night will look like an antitrust reform measure in the last House of Congress.[41] And I'll bet you my head against anything in sight that we can deliver the goods.

Fran.: Don't run those cheap bluffs on me. I will take the bet, however, for I like a little sport and will consider that your head is already up and in the hands of my executioner. My throne against your head that you can't deliver the goods.

Doo.: Taken.

>[*Duet. Fest. and Lou:*]
>   <u>Two Hearts that Beat in one Ragout</u>
>
>*Fest.:*
>Oh tender maid of Timbuctoo,
>Accept my burning love for you.
>Although your face has been my doom,
>It cheers me in the hour of gloom.
>*Lou:*
>Oh banished Prince of Timbuctoo,
>I'd gladly go to pot with you.
>'Tis sweet, 'tis sweet to die with you,
>Two hearts that beat in one ragout.
>   *Chorus:*
>   Two hearts that beat in one ragout.
>
>*Fest.:*
>From north, from south, from west, from east,
>They gather for the human feast.
>*Lou:*
>'Tis naught I care for mere life's loss,
>When served with you in Tartar sauce.
>   *Chorus:*
>   When served in Tartar sauce.
>
>*Fest.:*
>Behold those lank expectant coons,
>Are polishing their wooden spoons,
>And as they take us off the fire,
>We'll be doused with Worcestershire.
>   *Chorus:*
>   We'll be doused with Worcestershire.

Doo.: To Natives.
Last call for dinner, will you join?
Spareribs, cutlets, tenderloin,
Although too much will make you some sick.
White meat, dark meat, neck, or drumstick.
Will you feast upon her eyes,
With relish a la Paradise?
Would you fellows barbecue,
This tender maid of Timbuctoo?
   Chorus and Natives:
   You bet your life we'll barbecue,
   This tender maid of Timbuctoo.

Lou:
My heart warms up to you.
Fest.:
It will before we're through.
Both:
I long to strike the stew.
Bring on your barbecue.
'Tis sweet to die with you,
Two hearts in one ragout.
   Chorus:
   Two hearts in one ragout.
Fest.:
They'll feed us to their friends,
And all our hopes are dashed,
Lou:
And then our odds and ends,
For breakfast will be hashed.

Fran.: [*Taking Fest. aside.*] Give up the love so far beneath you and be mine. I offer you life, liberty, myself, the throne.

Fest.: Sings.

> I'd rather on a red hot spit,
> > Roast with my Lou,
> Than on a regal throne to sit,
> > With such a thing as you.

Fran.: [*Mounting the throne, in a rage as the seismograph begins to vibrate.*] You have staked all and lost. Where is the darkening of the moon you promised? Is it a little late or have you got cold feet?

Doo.: [*To Orn.*] Give her some hot air and play for time.

Orn.: [*To Doo.*] Go to your kennel and lie down. If you butt in now, all is lost. As you value your life, keep your hands off this eclipse and let me run it. It only lacks a few minutes of the time. [*Wireless instrument begins to click.*]

Doo.: There comes the Hennessey dispatch. We're saved.

Herald: [*Taking tape off the instrument.*] Your Majesty, this dispatch is for you. [*Hands it to Fran.*]

Fran.: [*Reading.*] To her Majesty, the Queen of Timbuctoo. [*To crowd.*] Ah, I am recognized by the other powers! [*Reading.*] "It is my painful duty to officially inform you that the destruction of the world takes place tonight. Roosevelt, President. By John Hay, Secretary of State."[42] [*Staggering to her feet.*] What can this mean? Pshaw! Only a weak invention of the enemy. Tell the head chef to begin operations at once. Tell the native band to play "The Heart Boiled Down" and "Let the Feast be Prepared"! Kindle the fires. [*Natives place wood under the pots.*] Mr. Markus, will you kindly preside as toastmaster?

Doo.: [*To Orn.*] If my watch is right the hour is at hand. Face her and run your bluff at this very moment.

Orn.: [*Approaching the throne.*] The time is at hand when I must fulfill the pledge. Let the face of the moon be darkened for the sins of the ruler of Timbuctoo. [*Waves his hand at the moon.*] 'Tis my command. [*The face of the moon begins to darken.*] Darkness for the whole earth. A gloom to wrap the world. [*Darkness increases.*]

Doo.: [*To the natives.*] To your knees, you misguided wretches, or you will never again see the light of day. [*Several of the natives grovel before Doo. and hand him large wads of money.*]

Orn.: [*To Doo.*] Please, don't butt in this time if you love me. You'll surely spoil the whole thing.

Doo.: Hush, Dan, and watch these cattle cough up the conscience money. These are the ward politicians I gave these greenbacks to buy votes with. They sunk every dollar and now they are coughin' it up. We'll git back every cint and maybe some more on top. [*Natives continue to throw wads of money at Doo. while the darkness increases.*]

Fran.: Have I been tricked? [*Consults her almanac.*] This almanac has no eclipse scheduled for tonight. Heavens! This almanac has today as Thursday when it's really Friday. As I live, this is a last year's edition bound in this year's cover. I'll sue the patent medicine company for damages.[43] [*Sinks on the steps of the throne.*]

Doo.: [*To Fran.*] Your Majesty, what do ye think of our eclipse?

Fran.: I fear it's mine. [*Collapses.*]

Doo.: Now's the time to abdicate. I have your San Francisco record. It just came by the wireless.

Fran.: [*Recovering.*] Give it to me straight. What is it?

Doo.: Ye were a witness in the Fair will case.[44]

Fran.: Oh my God, has it come to this? Life seemed too sweet to last, until I had the luck to bang up against my fearful past here in Timbuctoo. [*Collapses and falls at the foot of the throne, her crown rolling away from her.*]

Doo.: Everything's comin' our way. [*Flash of lighting and roll of thunder.*] Listen to that! Oh, but this is hot stuff! [*Natives grovel in the dust before Orn. and pray with their foreheads hitting the ground.*]

        Song. Natives:
The sky is like a funeral pall.
The gathering darkness covers all.
Come light, come day, come seven, come 'leven.
Oh, save us from the wrath of heaven.

Fest.: [*To Orn.*] Give me your hand, old boy. You have pulled off this eclipse, not exactly to the Queen's taste, but certainly to ours. [*They shake hands.*]
Lou: [*To Orn.*] Take this and it goes if they see it. [*Embraces and kisses him.*]
Fest.: Give him one for me. He's earned it. [*Another roll of thunder. At each thunder clap natives rush up to Doo. and shell out more money.*]
Doo.: These are queer weather conditions. A crash of thunder and a shower of greenbacks. A roll of thunder and more rolls of greenbacks. [*To the natives.*] Git a move on now if ye expect to live another minute.
Orn.: Mr. Dooley was kind enough to give me this hugely successful eclipse. I now hand it over to you, Prince Festicus, as its rightful owner and with it the throne of Timbuctoo. Accept it as a souvenir of our acquaintance. I would suggest that you take advantage of the situation and play the eclipse for all it's worth. The totality is about over and you can depend upon its lighting up from this on.
Fest.: [*Advancing to natives.*] Grovel in the dust if you want this pall of darkness lifted. [*Drawing sword.*] To your knees, caitiffs. Abase yourselves or die.

Doo.: That's the business. Crow 'em to the ropes. [*Natives continue to abase themselves.*]

Lou: Salute the new King, you tarriers.[45] [*Suddenly taking Miss Primrose aside.*] Say Priscill, will you do me a favor?

Prim.: Certainly.

Lou: It's the custom in this country when a King takes the throne and a bride, that the bride names a couple to stand up with her. It's the law of the land and all must obey.

Prim.: Indeed. Well, haven't I obeyed all the laws of this strange land so far? Look at this costume I'm wearing all because it was the royal edict. I guess I can stand almost anything after this.

Lou: You must marry Orndorff, the hustling American, and after the wedding you must come and keep house with us.

Prim.: Oh, but this is sudden. [*Lou turns to go.*] Don't rush off, I accept.

Lou: I was just starting to tell Orndorff that you had accepted. I've already talked to him. [*Joins the hands of Orn. and Prim.*]

Doo.: For onst I won't butt in. Say, but this is great! Come git a move on, Festy, and take the throne before it gits cool. [*Fest. and Lou ascend the steps of throne and stand together. Natives crowd up and continue to make obeisance.*] They make a fine couple, those two. Dan, allow me to congratulate ye on yer good luck. I had me eye on that same girl but I'll not interfere. There's lots of 'em left over there. [*Nods to Sextet.*]

Song. Sextet:
<u>Welcome Sweet Triumph's Hour</u>

Welcome sweet triumph's hour,
    With joy entrancing.
The heavens have ceased to lower,
    With moonbeams dancing.

So feel no longer sour,
> At fate's beguiling,
You've shown them all your power,
> And come up smiling.

So take your crown and throne,
> With good luck laden,
Timbuctoo's all your own,
> Likewise the maiden.

[*During the singing the light increases and at the close, Lou places the crown on the head of Fest. amid the shouts of the populace. The moonlight sends a shaft of dazzling splendor upon the couple on the throne while Fest. holds his sword aloft.*]

Doo.: It really looks now as if we had won the trick and the new government is well under way. All we need now is a Roosevelt big stick[46] to make us respected all over South Africa. Let's all drink to the health of the lovely couple up there on the top of the throne.

Drinking Song. Whole company:

Here's laughter and here's mirth,
With joy to all the earth,
> And good long life to you,
As we the goblet raise,
Here's health to those brave days,
> We've spent in Timbuctoo.

Although a costlier wine,
May flow at pleasure's shrine,
      The best the world e'er knew,
Is in your glasses here,
So raise another cheer,
      For dear old Timbuctoo.

An odor like the rose,
Is born where e'er it flows,
      And stirs this jolly crew,
And touched by memory's finger,
The wakened chords will linger,
      That sing of Timbuctoo.

It would not be surprising,
If when the sun was rising,
      Our revels are not through.
And while the foam is sinking,
We'd still be drinking, drinking,
      To dear old Timbuctoo.

[*Curtain.*]

End of Act Third.

THE END.

Notes

1. The line has been emended for obvious reasons from its original form: "If half the outside world but knew."

2. "Pink teas" was the term for light social gatherings, often attended by ladies. "Tan games" probably refers to games of fan tan, a card game of Chinese origin that is generally used for gambling. "Bucket shops" refers both to fraudulent brokerage establishments that delayed orders so that brokers could profit by what the customer was made to lose on the rise or fall of stock prices, and to saloons that sold drinks (e.g., beer) in buckets.

3. A finish fight was a fight that ended only when one participant either gave up or was disabled, as opposed to fights according to rules and with timed rounds, and which could be won or lost on points.

4. The line originally read, "Enter Markus dressed in black tights and claw hammer battered plug hat." It has been emended to give "claw hammer" its nominal meaning of a swallow-tailed coat. A plug hat was a man's high silk hat.

5. "Divil a bit" is the first of several amusing linguistic incongruities in the text, usually consisting—as in this case—of Irish vernacular spoken by natives.

6. Apparently, Davis regarded Mendocino County as synonymous with rural unsophistication.

7. "Dolly Green," etc. Names of songs and poems popular at the time of writing.

8. "Long green" is a slang term for money, i.e., dollar bills.

9. "Hub" is short for "hubby" or "hubbie," i.e., husband.

10. In 1905, the risqué character of this song would have pushed propriety to its limits. Omitted from this version is a next stanza crossed out in the copyrighted version that, with its more overt implication of adultery, would have transgressed those limits:

> And every day when the sea was bright,
> To meet that diver was my delight,
> While my hubbie sitting upon the shore,
> Remarked that sea bathing was quite a bore.

11. Andrew Carnegie (1835–1919) was a spectacularly successful American businessman whose ventures included steel mills and bridge-building companies. In 1901, these companies were combined into a single corporation, United States Steel, and Carnegie retired from business and henceforth devoted himself to

philanthropic enterprises. Davis inaccurately treats Carnegie as if he were still in charge of the corporation.

12. A "Midway show" referred to an exhibition or entertainment attached to a fair. The term probably derived from the World's Columbian Exposition held in Chicago in 1892. Part of the exposition grounds was known as the Midway and featured such shows.

13. This and the next two stanzas allude to the monopolies, trusts, and disreputable business and commercial practices whose growing influence had recently begun to be addressed by federal legislation. Davis accuses Carnegie Steel of having helped start the Boer War.

14. "Dust"—gold dust, i.e., money.

15. "Build a head on him"—slang for put a bump on his head, i.e., hit him hard on the head.

16. The Vanderbilt family fortune established by Cornelius Vanderbilt (1794–1877) had been inherited by the turn of the century by his grandsons, including Frederick William Vanderbilt (1856–1938).

17. The Exposition Universelle de Paris took place in 1900. This reference also helps date the manuscript.

18. By "cathode ray," Davis perhaps means X ray. The attachment that makes thought reading possible is a reference to *The Psychoscope*, a play by Rollin M. Daggett and Joseph T. Goodman that was briefly but famously performed in Virginia City, Nevada, in 1872. The psychoscope of the play was an invention that supposedly visibly projected one's thoughts on a screen. Davis never saw the play but he obviously knew about it and must have been impressed by the idea of the invention, for in 1880 he referred to it as the "cycroscope" in an essay on Comstock drama, and here uses the idea for his own play. In both versions of the operetta he further misspells it as "sycroscope." This edition of the Stoddard text restores the correct spelling.

19. In March 1903 John Pierpont Morgan (1837–1913), a famous and influential American financier, had blamed a downturn in the economy on "undigested securities" in the financial markets. This allusion helps to date the play.

20. Joshing reference to President Theodore Roosevelt's well-known fondness for hunting, in America and overseas, and his activities in establishing state and national parks.

21. Dooley delivers a riposte to the king's racial insinuation that his mother might have lived loosely in Timbuctoo with his own deft innuendo that some of the women of the king's court could have had amorous affairs with Dooley's father.

22. "Puts you dead next" is clarified in the following lines as meaning "alerts you to the plot."

23. This burlesque of a Supreme Court composed of gorillas is capped by its phrase "our usual promptness," whose implied criticism of the slowness of the American court system is made explicit in Markus's next lines.

24. An allusion to Anthony Trollope's *La Mere Bauche* (1861): "It never seemed to impede the rigid punctilious propriety of his movements."

25. Allusions to notorious events then in the news.

26. "Buffalo," besides possibly being an allusion to a citizen of a major city in New York State was also a term for a rough and burly man. In other words, "Are you up to the job?"

27. "Drummer" was a term for a traveling salesman.

28. Sir Thomas Lipton (1850–1931), who made a fortune as an importer and retailer of tea and is now known for a brand of tea that bears his name, was also a famous yachting enthusiast and competed for the America Cup in 1899, 1901, and 1903. The latter date may be another clue to the dating of the manuscript.

29. On 17 March 1897 Carson City hosted a heavyweight championship boxing match between Jim Corbett and Robert Fitzsimmons. Sam Davis and his wife were part of the organizing planners. Perhaps due to satisfactory arrangements, subsequent world championship boxing matches were also held in Carson City.

30. Potter Palmer (1826–1902) was a prominent Chicago capitalist and real estate promoter. He helped found the department store that became Marshall Field's, and was especially influential in developing Chicago's State Street for business and the lakefront area north of the Chicago River for expensive residences. It appears that Hennessey opposed Palmer.

31. The cakewalk was a popular American dance step of the late nineteenth and early twentieth centuries.

32. These lines pun on various meanings of "do." "Hard to do" means hard to fool. "To do him" means to do him in, i.e., kill him.

33. "Carte" and "tierce" are technical terms from fencing. A carte is a palm-up thrust toward an opponent's breast, and tierce is a position from which a fencer can either parry or thrust.

34. Women earned the right to vote in Colorado in 1893. At the next election, the Democrats, who had supported their enfranchisement, were largely defeated.

35. "I opened a roughhouse," i.e., "I threw a punch."

36. Dooley is here expressing a current American prejudice against Asians, particularly Chinese. Congress passed its first racial segregation law, against Chinese, in 1882.

37. Dooley mangles the name "jujitsu," a Japanese technique of self-defense.

38. Possibly Davis meant Ujiji, an African town that was occasionally in the news in the late nineteenth and early twentieth centuries. If so, however, Davis would have picked it for its exotic name as its location on Lake Tanganyika places

it more than twenty-seven hundred miles east of Timbuctoo. But geographical accuracy is not a main concern of this operetta.

39. A reference to New York's famous Four Hundred—the most elite people of the city and, hence, also the most influential and socially eminent.

40. William Jennings Bryan was a leading advocate of free silver and ran unsuccessfully for president in 1896 and again in 1900 on a platform of increased coinage of silver dollars.

41. An ironic allusion to the lack of Congressional enthusiasm for President Roosevelt's antitrust reform bills.

42. John Hay (1838–1905) was U.S. Secretary of State from 1898 until his death.

43. Patent medicine companies frequently printed and distributed almanacs as advertising promotions.

44. One of the most notorious legal scandals of the turn of the century was the long contest, ending in 1902, over the will of James Fair, a former Silver King of the Comstock and U.S. Senator from Nevada. After his death in 1894, a number of women claimed either to have been quietly married to him, or to have had children fathered by him.

45. "Tarrier" is an old-fashioned term for someone who tarries or delays, or who causes delay.

46. Theodore Roosevelt was fond of quoting the African proverb "Walk softly and carry a big stick," which soon became associated with his foreign policy as president.

Index

Abbott, Bud, 19
Ah Sin (Twain and Harte), 10, 19

Barrett, Lawrence, 9
Beethoven, Ludwig van, 66, 126n28
Beggar's Opera, The (Gay), 131, 136, 141
Belasco, David, 2, 14
Bernhardt, Sarah, 11
Bierce, Ambrose, 132, 133
Boer War, 136
Bohemian's Blunder, The (Davis), 132
Boston, 2, 136
Boucicault, Dion, 9, 11, 13, 14, 15
Brennan, Walter, 16
Bright, William, 138
Bryan, William Jennings, 212, 224n40
Buntline, Ned, 3

Campbell, Bartley, 2
Carnegie Steel, 136, 137, 139, 145, 148, 222n13
Carnegie, Andrew, 155, 221–22n11
Carson City, Nevada, 132, 133, 135, 138, 223n29
Carson City *Morning Appeal*, 132
Chaumont, Celine, 12
Chicago, 1, 136, 139, 222n12, 223n30
Cody, William F. (Buffalo Bill), 3
Cole, Robert, 138
Corbett, Jim, 223n29
Costello, Lou, 19

Crabtree, Lotta, 12
Crockett, Davy, 3

Daggett, Rollin Mallory, 132, 144n5, 222n18
Daly, Augustin, 2, 9, 10, 12
Davis, Sam, 1, 2, 4, 5, 6, 131–44, 224n6, 225n11, 225n18, 226n38
De Quille, Dan, 132, 144n5
Dickens, Charles, 3
Doten, Alfred, 144n5
Dunne, Finley Peter, 139

Euclid, 28, 125n6

Fair, James, 135, 137, 224n44
Fairbanks, Douglas, 15–16
Fitch, Clyde, 2
Fitzsimmons, Robert, 223n29
Frohman, Charles, 13, 14

Garner, James, 16
Gay, John, 131, 136, 137, 141
Gilbert, William S., 131, 140, 141
Goodman, Joe, 132, 144n5, 222n18
Goodwin, C. C., 132, 144n5
Gudde, Erwin C., 138

Harte, Anna, 2, 11, 13, 14, 15, 18
Harte, Bret, 1, 2, 4, 5, 6, 9–20, 132
Harte, Frank, 13
Hawks, Howard, 16

Hay, John, 11, 215, 224n42
Herbert, Victor, 141
Hitchcock-Coit, Eliza (Lillie), 126n27
Homer, 28, 125n7
Howard, Bronson, 14
Howells, W. D., 1, 9, 11
Hyde, Stuart, 2

Irving, Washington, 4

James, 1, 3, 4, 5, 9, 18
Johnson, James Weldon, 138

Kelly, Grace, 16
King, Clarence, 11
King of Timbuctoo, The (Mumford), 138
Kohlman, Chas., 142

Lipton, Sir Thomas, 190, 223n28
London, 10, 11, 14

McCarthy, Denis, 132
McCloskey, James J., 2
Manet, Edouard, 127n52
Mathew, Theobald, 28, 125n5
Mayo, Frank, 3
Mighels, Henry, 132
Mighels, Nellie Verrill, 132
Mikado, The (Gilbert and Sullivan), 140
Miller, Joaquin, 2
Moody, William Vaughn, 2
Morgan, J. P., 165, 222n19
Mumford, Leon O., 138

New York, 2, 9, 10, 12, 13, 14, 15

New York Times, 10
New York Tribune, 9

Overland Monthly, 9, 10

Palmer, Potter, 191, 193, 223n30
Paris, 11, 12, 13, 222n17
Pemberton, T. Edgar, 10
Philadelphia, 136
Pickford, Mary, 16
Pleasant, Mary Ellen "Mammy," 139

Reagan, Ronald, 16
Richmond, Rosalind, 141–42
Roosevelt, Theodore, 137, 165, 191, 215, 219, 222n20, 224n41, 224n46
Russell, Annie, 10
Russell, Lillian, 138

Samary, Jeanne, 12
San Francisco, 1, 135
San Francisco *Daily Evening Bulletin*, 126
Sculptor's Daughter, The (Davis), 132
Sousa, John Philip, 141
St. Louis, 1
Stoddard, Sylvia Crowell, 133–34
Stoddard Collection, 133, 134, 142
Sullivan, Sir Arthur, 131, 140, 141

Thomas, Augustus, 2
Toole, John L., 15
Townsend, James W. E., 144n5
Triple Plated Honeymoon: A Chinese Comedy, The (Davis), 134
Trollope, Anthony, 223n24
Trollope, Frances, 3

Twain, Mark, 1, 3, 4, 10, 11, 132, 140
Two Men of Sandy Bar (Harte), 10
Tyler, Royall, 3

Vanderbilt, Cornelius, 222n16
Vanderbilt, Frederick William, 163, 222n16
Velde, Mme Van de, 10–11, 13, 15, 16, 17, 19
Virginia City, Nevada, 1, 132, 134, 222n18

Watrous, Charles, 13, 19
Wharton, Edith, 3, 4, 5
Wister, Owen, 2
Worth, Charles Francis, 88, 126n45